CORPUS SCRIPTORUM DE MUSICA

GILBERT REANEY
General Editor

THE ANONYMOUS COMPENDIUM MUSICES
Venice, 1499–1597

Edited by
DAVID CRAWFORD

AMERICAN INSTITUTE OF MUSICOLOGY
ARMEN CARAPETYAN
Director

CORPVS SCRIPTORVM DE MVSICA

33

ANONYMVS
COMPENDIVM MVSICES
Venetiis, 1499–1597

Edidit
DAVID CRAWFORD

AMERICAN INSTITUTE OF MUSICOLOGY
HÄNSSLER-VERLAG
1985
68.330

Hänssler-Verlag, D-7303 Neuhausen-Stuttgart
Order No. 68.330
ISBN 3-7751-0964-1

TABLE OF CONTENTS

LIST OF ILLUSTRATIONS

PREFACE

The anonymous *Compendium musices* holds a special place in the history of music theory, not only because its first edition was an incunabulum, but also because the text enjoyed special popularity among the Venetian presses; it seems to have run about 29 editions from 1499 to 1597. Evidently it was the most frequently published theory treatise in Renaissance Italy. The *Compendium* was also exceptional because it received papal endorsement; a decree by none other than the music-loving Pope Leo X promoted its use. The purpose of the present study is limited to clarifying the text and its sources. The *Compendium* has received almost no prior musicological attention, so an article discussing its historical role is being prepared for publication separately.

I am grateful to the Rackham Graduate School of the University of Michigan for a research fellowship which enabled me to conduct the European research during the summer of 1981. The American Philosophical Society also provided a grant to support this project. A large number of librarians, both in the U.S. and Europe, cheerfully responded to my requests for help; their institutions are identified in the list of sources given below. Among colleagues who provided special help, Professors Howard Brown, Ruth Craig, Charles Hamm, Albert Seay, and Thomas Warburton deserve special thanks. A graduate student, Bruce Flamma, doublechecked bibliographical citations and also prepared the musical examples.

Some modern aids alleviated the clerical toil inherent in this kind of work. All the preparation was facilitated by automated word processing; this method also produced, without extra labor, an index of technical words and their contexts, thereby assisting the search for quotations from earlier treatises. Gregory's Scribe, a micro-computer program co-authored by Jon Zeeff and myself, copied the musical examples. Finally, one edition, Giunta's *Sacerdotale* of 1585, came to my attention through the OCLC library network data base. To the Computing Center and the School of Music, University of Michigan, go my thanks for these admirable tools.

THE SOURCES

References to secondary sources, limited to the most informative items, will be abbreviated as follows:

Adams	Adams, Herbert, *Catalogue of Books Printed on the Continent of Europe, 1501–1600, in Cambridge Libraries* (Cambridge, 1967), 2 vols.
Ales	Ales, Anatole, *Bibliothèque Liturgique; Description des Livres de Liturgie imprimés aux XVe et XVIe Siècles faisent Partie de la Bibliothèque des S. A. R. Mgr Charles-Louis de Bourbon* (New York, 1970, first published 1878).
BM *GenCat*	British Museum, *General Catalogue of Printed Books* (London, 1962–1966), 263 vols.
Bohatta	Bohatta, Hans, *Katalog der liturgischen Drucke des XV. und XVI. Jahrhunderts in der herzogl. Parma'schen Bibliothek in Schwarzau am Steinfeld, N.Oe.* (Vienna, 1909–1910), 2 vols.
Camerini	Camerini, Paolo, *Annali dei Giunti,* vol. I (in two parts), *Venezia* (Florence, 1962).
RISM-Ecr	Lesure, François (ed.), *Écrits imprimés concernant la musique* (München, Duisburg, 1971), B VI of *Répertoire internationale des sources musicales,* 2 vols.
Essling	Essling, Victor, Le Prince d', *Les livres à figures venitiens de la fin du XVe siècle et du commencement du XVIe, 1469–1525* (Paris and Florence, 1907–1914).
Gaspari	Gaspari, Gaetano, *Catalogo della Biblioteca del Liceo*

Musicale di Bologna (Bologna, 1890), 5 vols.

Mansell	Mansell Information/Publishing Limited and American Library Association, *The National Union Catalog, Pre-1956 Imprints* (London, 1968–1980), 685 vols.
NYPL	The New York Public Library, Reference Department, *Dictionary Catalog of the Music Collection* (Boston, 1964), 33 vols.
Pancini	Pancini, Paolo, *Venezia, Santa Maria della Consolazione, Catalogo del Fondo Musicale,* in *Bibliotheca Musicae* VI (Milan, 1969).
Rava	Rava, Carlo, *Supplement à Max Sander, Le Livre à Figures in Italien de la Renaissance* (Milan, 1969).
Sander	Sander, Max, *Le Livre à Figures Italien Depuis 1467 jusqu'à 1530* (New York, 1941).

One of the challenges in this project has been bibliographical, for the books containing the *Compendium* pose difficulties for librarians and bibliographers. Although the printed book of the sixteenth century deserves much more attention, the ecclesiastical books are especially neglected. The problem is compounded because these books received much use, sometimes thereby losing title pages and colophons. The following booklists represent progress in understanding the *Compendium's* bibliographical background, but some questions still remain unanswered.

One case, a *Cantorinus* printed by Giunta in 1540, is so complex that it deserves special discussion, so it can serve here as an illustration of the complications involved. Camerini's bibliography of Giunta's work lists only one edition for 1540, but RISM-Ecr II seems to list two Giunta editions of the *Compendium,* one on page 926 under the title *Compendium* (83 folios) and another on page 923 under the title *Cantorinus* (88 folios). The story begins with my visit to the Euing Music Library, Glasgow University, which RISM-Ecr reports as owning both books. Only one book of 1540 seems to be there, and no evidence emerges that the library owned a second book in the past. The next stop, the British Library, also promised to reveal the two different books; both titles are entered in RISM-Ecr and in BM *GenCat* as well. But the two entries in BM *GenCat* refer to the same call number, an item which the library staff cannot now find; they hypothesize that it was lost during the bombing of World War II. According to RISM-Ecr, one hope remained to find the edition entitled *Cantorinus,* the Pendlebury Music Library at Cambridge University. The library staff there, and the catalogue by Adams as well, affirms only one edition, the one titled *Compendium.* These experiences seem to agree with Camerini, who knew of one edition. The volume is actually in two parts, the first part a theoretical introduction (the *Compendium*) and the second a small monastic chantbook (the *Cantorinus*). Confusion may have resulted from the fact that each part has its own title page. Some cataloguers appear to have entered the edition under the first title page, *Compendium;* others used the later one, *Cantorinus.* A second 1540 edition may have been born during the failure of a cross-indexing system.

I studied two other copies of this edition, and the one at the Biblioteca Civica Angelo Mai, Bergamo, matches the one at Glasgow. However, a book at the Biblioteca Nazionale Centrale in Rome, found by accident because published bibliographies have overlooked it, complicates the picture. Here is a Giunta book of 1540 whose physical properties corresponded to the other two that I consulted, but its musical examples were more accurate. We might speculate that the faulty version was stopped in midrun when errors were discovered, the press then continuing with a revise. It is obviously unrealistic to try to locate and verify the readings in every surviving copy of every edition, but such a task might provide more insight into the publication history of the *Compendium.*

The editions identified thus far are listed below, along with abbreviations for each. Citations of secondary sources are selective, limited to the more informative items. Names of printing establishments are Italianized.[1] Unless otherwise indicated, every edition has been consulted *in situ.*

Published as an independent treatise

The first printing of the *Compendium* was as an independent treatise, issued in these three quarto editions:

T499 [*Compendium musices*]. Venice, Giovanni Battista Sessa [il Vecchio], 1499.[2]

4°, 8 ff., 184 x 135, print field 165 x 127, black ink only, 40 lines per page.

RISM-Ecr II, 925; Sander #2074.

Copy consulted: Bodleian Library, Oxford University.

T505 *Tractatus musices.*[3] Venice, Giovanni Battista Sessa [il Vecchio], [c. 1505].

4°, 8 ff., 216 x 159, print field 156 x 125, black ink only, 39 lines per page.

Gaspari I, 262; Sander #7347 and plate 260; Mansell 599, 354; RISM-Ecr II, 925.

Copy consulted: Newberry Library, Chicago.

[1] The standard bibliographer's form "Giunta" is retained, but in all other cases I follow the name forms in Ester Pastorello, *Tipografi, editori, librai, a Venezia nel secolo XVI* (Florence, 1924).

[2] This edition has no title or title page and there probably never was one, since the treatise presently consists of two sheets cut and folded into a quarto pamphlet of eight folios. The printer and date are given in the explicit, which also records, *Explicit musices non inutile Compendium.* RISM-Ecr lists a copy of T499 at the Library of Congress, but comparison with the copy of T499 at Oxford shows that the Library of Congress copy is actually T505.

[3] A new heading above the Guidonian hand, *Tractatus musices,* serves as title on folio 1r. The wording of the explicit matches that of T499.

T509 *Compendium musices confectum ad faciliorem introductionem discentium.*[4] Venice, Simone De Luere, 1509.

4°, 8 ff., 208 x 155, print field 160 x 125, black ink only, 44 lines per page.

BM *GenCat* 42, col. 648; Sander #2075; Mansell 118, 205; NYPL 7, 484; RISM-Ecr II, 925.

Copy consulted: New York Public Library, New York City.

Published as a preface to the "Cantorinus"

In 1513, Lucantonio Giunta undertook the printing of a small monastic chantbook known as the *Cantorinus.* Although he appears not to have published the *Compendium* before this time, he settled upon the *Compendium* as a preface to the songbook. Over the next half-century Venetian printers continued to combine the two materials into one volume, and here is a list of the editions known to me.

C513 *Compendium musices confectum ad faciliorem instructionem cantum choralem discentium: necnon ad introductionem huius libelli: qui Cantorinus intitulatur: omnibus diuino cultui deditis per utilis et necessarius: ut in tabula hic immediate sequenti latius apparet.* Venice, Lucantonio Giunta, 1513.

8°, 120 ff., 158 x 106, print field 102 x 70, red and black ink, 30 lines per page. The *Compendium* appears on folios 2v to 16r.

RISM-Ecr II, 925; Essling, p. 355; BM *GenCat* 33, col. 454 and 42, col. 648; Mansell 118, 205; Sander #1602; Camerini pt. I, 155; Gaspari II, 6–7.

Copy consulted: University of Michigan, Ann Arbor, Michigan.[5]

[4] *Tractatus musices* continues to appear as a title above the Guidonian hand on folio 1v.

[5] This copy is not listed in RISM-Ecr.

C538 [Title matches C513]. Venice, Pietro Liechtenstein, 1538.

8°, 16 + 88 ff., 155 x 104, print field 113 x 77, red and black ink, 30 lines per page. The *Compendium* appears in the first 16 folios.

RISM-Ecr I, 926; BM *GenCat* 33, col. 454; Gaspari II, 7; Mansell 118, 205.

Copy consulted: Civico Museo Bibliografico Musicale, Bologna.

C540A *Cantorinus ad eorum instructionem: qui cantum ad chorum pertinentem breviter et quam facillime discere concupiscunt: et non clericis modo, sed omnibus etiam divino cultui deditus, per quam utilis et necessarius in quo facilis modus est additus ad discendam manum, ac tonos psalmorum, ...* Venice, Lucantonio Giunta, 1540.

8°, 16 + 87 + 1 ff., 157 x 100, print field 115 x 80, 31 lines per page, red and black ink. The *Compendium* occurs in the first 16 folios.

Camerini pt. II, 322; RISM-Ecr II, 923; BM *GenCat* 33, col. 454.

Copies consulted: Euing Music Library, Glasgow University; Biblioteca Civica Angelo Mai, Bergamo.

C540B [A more correct version of C540A; see discussion, p. 14 above].

Copy consulted: Biblioteca Nazionale Centrale, Rome.

C549 [Title matches C513]. Venice, Pietro Liechtenstein, 1549.

8°, 16 + 87 ff., 154 x 103, print field 114 x 77, 31 lines per page, black and red ink. The first 16 folios contain the *Compendium.*

RISM-Ecr II, 926; BM *GenCat* 33, col. 454; Gaspari II, 7; Mansell 118, 205; Sander #2076.

Copy consulted: University of Michigan, Ann Arbor, Michigan.

C550 *Cantorinus ad eorum instructionem: qui cantum ad chorum pertinentem breviter & quam facillime discere concupiscunt: & non clericis modo, sed omnibus etiam diuino cultui deditis, perquam utilis, & necessarius. In quo facilis modus est additus ad discendam manum, ac tonos psalmorum: vt sequens Tabula indicabit. Nouissime castigatus, cui etiam addite sunt Letanie.* Venice, Eredi Lucantonio Giunta, 1550.

8°, 8 + 104 ff., 160 x 109, print field 140 x 87, red and black ink, 30 lines per page. The *Compendium* appears in the first 8 folios.

Camerini pt. I, 377; RISM-Ecr II, 923; BM *GenCat* 33, col. 454; Gaspari II, 5; NYPL 5, 323; Mansell 94, 244.

Copy consulted: Newberry Library, Chicago.

C566 *Cantorinus pro his, qui cantum ad chorum pertinentem, breuiter et quam facillime discere concupiscunt: & non clericis modo, sed omnibus etiam divino cultui deditis, perquam utilis, et necessarius. In quo facilis modus est additus ad discendam manum: ac tonos psalmorum, vt sequens tabula indicabit. Novissime castigatus.* Venice, Eredi Lucantonio Giunta, 1566.[6]

8°, 8 + 104 ff., 160 x 103, print field 135 x 88, red

[6] Contrary to the information in RISM-Ecr and Mansell, no trace of this edition could be found at Indiana University when I visited there in August, 1980. The copy I consulted in Florence is not listed in RISM-Ecr. Also, if the listing in Robert G. Marshall, *Short-Title Catalog of Books Printed in Italy and of Books in Italian Printed Abroad, 1501–1600, Held in Selected North American Libraries* (Boston, 1970), I, 344, is correct, Giunta brought out two issues, rather than one, during 1566.

and black ink, 30 lines per page. The *Compendium* appears in the first 8 folios.

Camerini pt. I, 443–444; Gaspari II, 5; RISM-Ecr II, 923; Mansell 94, 244; BM *GenCat* 33, col. 455; NYPL 5, 323.

Copy consulted: Biblioteca Nazionale Centrale, Florence.

Published as part of a rituale

The majority of the editions of the *Compendium* is found in yet another branch of the Venetian book tradition: a large, general reference book for clergy, sometimes classed as a "Rituale." So far as I can learn, this tradition has not been the subject of modern systematic bibliography, and these editions did not find their way into RISM-Ecr. These books shed light on the execution of liturgy and other information needed by the clergy, and they also provide a useful collection of frequently needed chants. Mainstreams of this tradition subdivide into two parts, one a *Sacerdotale* in quarto, and the other a smaller book in octavo, *Familiaris Clericorum.* An early edition of the *Familiaris Clericorum* appeared in 1517, but this historic book does not contain the *Compendium.* (See page 28 below.)

The earliest Rituale containing the *Compendium,* then, was published in 1523. This is the first edition of a *Sacerdotale* compiled by a Venetian Dominican, Alberto Castellano (Castello, Castellani, or da Castello). Castellano compiled several important Venetian ecclesiastical imprints, one of which was a *Liber Pontificalis* (1520). This book, dedicated to Pope Leo X, was reprinted frequently throughout the century. His *Sacerdotale* was also intended for Pope Leo X. In a Breve of 1520, Leo X not only approved the book, but also decreed that, when it was published, its contents were to be observed by all ecclesiastical personnel.[7] The publication, however, took place in 1523, so the actual

[7] The text of this and other documents concerning the *Sacerdotale* is given in E. Cattaneo, "Il Rituale Romano di Alberto Castellani," *Miscellanea Liturgia in Onore di sua eminenza il Cardinale Giacomo Lercaro* II (Rome, 1967), 629–647; Cattaneo also lists the contents of the *Sacerdotale* and singles out other important studies on the subject. See also Marco Palma, "Castellano (da Castello), Alberto," *Dizionario Biografico degli Italiani,* 21 (Rome, 1978), 642–644.

dedication of the book went to Leo X's successor, Adrian VI.

Following is a list of consulted Rituales which contain the *Compendium.*

R523 *Liber Sacerdotalis nuperrime ex libris sancte Romane ecclesie et quarundam aliarum ecclesiarum: et ex antiquis codicibus apostolice bibliothece: et ex iurium sanctionibus et ex doctorum ecclesiasticorum scriptis ad Reuerendorum patrum sacerdotum parrochialium et aliarum curam habentium commodum collectus atque compositus: ac auctoritate Sanctissimi D. Domini nostri Leonis decimi approbatum . . .* [Castellano]. Venice, Melchiore Sessa [il Vecchio] e Pietro Dei Ravani, 1523.

4°, 8 + 367 ff., 266 x 140, print field 170 x 115, 36 lines per page, black and red ink. The *Compendium* appears on folios 334r to 344v.

Gaspari II, 10; Sander II, 680; BM *GenCat* 139, col. 507.

Copy consulted: Biblioteca Apostolica Vaticana.

R530 *Familiaris Clericorum Liber, nuper summa diligentia reformatus atque excusus, In quo reformando multa superflua sunt amota, multa uero curam animarum habentibus necessaria sunt addita, ad sacramentorum exhibitionem secundum ritum. S. Ro. Ecclesie ex antiquis sacrorum doctorum scriptis excerpta* . . . . Venice, Lucantonio Giunta, 1530.

8°, 16 + 281 ff., 150 x 105, print field 128 x 75, 33 lines per page, black and red ink. The *Compendium* appears on folios 211r to 222v.

Camerini pt. I, 238: Mansell 166, 344; Sander #2649; BM *GenCat* 139, col. 507.

Copy consulted: Princeton Theological Seminary, Princeton, New Jersey.

R537 [Title matches R523]. Venice, Vittore Dei Ravani e Compagni, 1537.

4°, 356 ff., 280 x 145, print field 179 x 117, 36 lines per page, black and red ink. The *Compendium* appears on folios 317r to 327r.

BM *GenCat* 139, col. 507.

Copy consulted: photocopy from the private library of Prof. Howard Brown.

R548 [Title matches R523]. Venice, Eredi Pietro Dei Ravani & Compagni, 1548.

4°, 4 + 351 + 1 ff., 217 x 160, print field 176 x 116, 36 lines per page, red and black ink. The *Compendium* appears on folios 317r to 327r.

No citations.

Copy consulted: Biblioteca Casanatense, Rome.

R554 *Sacerdotale iuxta s. Romane ecclesie et aliarum ecclesiarum ex apostolice bibliotece, ac sanctorum patrum iurium sanctionibus et ecclesiasticorum doctorum scriptis ad optatum commodum quorumcunque sacerdotum collectus, et omni nuper diligentia castigatus ac summorum Pontificum authoritate multoties approbatum . . .* [Castellano]. Venice, Eredi Pietro Dei Ravani & Compagni, 1554.

4°, 6 + 346 + 2 ff., 215 x 156, print field 175 x 110, 37 lines per page, red and black ink. The *Compendium* appears on folios 312r to 322r.

Rava, p. 87; BM *GenCat* 139, col. 507.

Copy consulted: Biblioteca Apostolica Vaticana.

R555 [Title matches R554]. Venice, Pietro Boselli, 1555.

4°, 4 + 331 + 1 ff., 219 x 162, print field 184 x 126, red and black ink. The *Compendium* appears on folios 299r to 308r.

Rava, p. 87; BM *GenCat* 139, col. 507.

Copy consulted: Biblioteca Nazionale Marciana, Venice.

R560 *Sacerdotale iuxta s. Romane ecclesie, et aliarum ecclesiarum collectum, et omni nuper diligentia castigatum . . . Canones etiam omnium excommunicationum additi sunt cum breui illarum et absoluta declaratione ex sacris doctoribus collecta. Lamentationes Hieremiae prophetae in hebdomada sancta ab vno vel duobus decantandae* . . . Venice, Giovanni Varisco e Compagni, 1560.

4°, 4 + 346 ff., 220 x 154, print field 175 x 114, 37 lines per page, black and red ink. The *Compendium* appears at folios 312r to 322r.

Gaspari II, 16; Adams I, 660.

Copy consulted: Biblioteca Apostolica Vaticana.

R564 *Sacerdotale ad consuetudinem s. Romane Ecclesie aliarumque ecclesiarum ex apostolice bibliothece, ac sanctorum patrium iurium sanctionibus, et ecclesiasticorum doctorum scriptis, ad optatum commodum quorumcunque sacerdotum, collectum: atque summorum pontificum authoritate multoties approbatum* . . . [Castellano]. Venice, Giovanni Varisco e Compagni, 1564.

4°,4 + 341 + 1 ff., 278 x 213, print field 212 x 150, 37 lines per page, red and black ink. The *Compendium* appears on folios 308v to 316v.

BM *GenCat* 139, col. 507; Bohatta II, #386.

Copy consulted: Biblioteca Apostolica Vaticana.

R567 [Title matches R564]. Venice, Pietro Liechtenstein, 1567.

4°, 4 + 328 ff., 220 x 165, print field 185 x 122, 39 lines per page, red and black ink. The *Compendium* appears on folios 295r to 304r.

Gaspari II, 16; BM *GenCat* 139, col. 508; Mansell 99, 554; Bohatta II, #387.

Copy consulted: Biblioteca Apostolica Vaticana.

R569 [Title matches R564]. Venice, Giovanni Varisco e Compagni, 1569.

4°, 4 + 340 ff., 210 x 154, print field 175 x 115, 37 lines per page, red and black ink. The *Compendium* appears on folios 306v to 315r.

BM *GenCat* 139, col. 508; Bohatta II. #388.

Copy consulted: Bodleian Library, Oxford University.

R576 *Sacerdotale ad consuetudinem S. Romanum Ecclesiae aliarumque ecclesiarum ex Apostolicae bibliotecae ac Sanctorum Patrum iurium sanctionibus, & ecclesiasticorum doctorum scriptis, ad optatum quorumcunque sacerdotum commodum, collectum: atqve svmmorvm pontificvm authoritate multoties approbatum: Summa nuper cura iuxta S. Tridentini Concilij . . .* [Castellano]. Venice, Guerra Fratelli e Soci, 1576.

4°, 4 + 372 ff. + 2, 240 x 150, print field 170 x 115, 37 lines per page, red and black ink. The *Compendium* appears on folios 319v to 328r.

Mansell 99, 554.

Copy consulted: University of Michigan, Ann Arbor, Michigan.

R579A [Title matches R576]. Venice, Domenico Nicolini, 1579.

4°, 4 + 375 + 1 ff., 208 x 155, print field 170 x 118, 37 lines per page, red and black ink. The *Compendium* appears on folios 319v to 328r.

BM *GenCat* 139, col. 508.

Copy consulted: British Library, London.

R579B [Title matches R576]. Giovanni Battista Sessa [il Giovane], 1579.

4°, 4 + 375 + 1 ff., 215 x 160, print field 169 x 115, 37 lines per page, red and black ink. The *Compendium* appears on folios 319v to 328 r.

Mansell 99, 554.

Copy consulted: Catholic University of America, Washington, D.C.

R585A [Title matches R576]. Venice, Domenico Nicolini, 1585.

4°, 4 + 375 + 1 ff., 215 x 160, print field 180 x 115, 37 lines per page. The *Compendium* appears on folios 319v to 328r.

Adams I, 660; Ales, p. 277; BM *GenCat* 139, col. 508; Gaspari II, 16; Bohatta II, #389.

Copy consulted: University of Minnesota, Minneapolis.

R585B [Title matches R576]. Venice, Giunta, 1585.

4°, 4 + 375 + 1 ff., 228 x 165, print field 172 x 120, 37 lines per page, red and black ink. The *Compendium* appears on folios 319v to 328r.

OCLC library network data base.

Copy consulted: photocopy from Syracuse University, Syracuse, New York.

R587 *Sacerdotale ad S. R. Ecclesiam consuetudinem Sacri Concilii Tridentini sanctionibus, Summorum Pontificum constitutionibus, sanctorumque, Patrum, ac doctorum Scriptis collectum. Nuper emendatioribus typis . . .* Venice, Giunta, 1587.

4°, 4 + 375 + 1 ff., 244 x 176, print field 230 x 130, 36 lines per page, red and black ink. The *Compendium* appears on folios 348v to 357r.

Camerini pt. II, 139; BM *GenCat* 139, col. 508.

Copy consulted: Biblioteca Apostolica Vaticana.

R588 *Sacerdotale Secvndum Vsvm S. R. Ecclesiae Aliarumque Ecclesiarum, ex Apostolicae bibliothecae, Councilii Tridentini ac sanctorum patrum iurum sanctionibus, et Ecclesiasticorum Doctorum Scriptis, ad optatum commodum quorumcunque sacerdotum collectum, . . .* [Castellano]. Venice, Giovanni Varisco & Paganini (dei) Paganino, 1588.

4°, 4 + 295 ff., 242 x 176, print field 198 x 140, 42 lines per page, red and black ink. The *Compendium* appears on folios 257r to 363v.

No citations.

Copy consulted: Biblioteca Nazionale Marciana, Venice.

R596 [Title matches R576]. Venice, Giovanni Battista Sessa e Giovanni Bernardo Sessa, Fratelli, 1596.

4°, 4 + 375 + 1 ff., 258 x 158, print field 172 x 116, 37 lines per page, red and black ink. The *Compendium* appears on folios 318v to 328r.

Mansell 99, 554.

Copy consulted: Biblioteca Apostolica Vaticana.

R597 [Title matches R576]. Venice, Giovanni Battista Sessa e Giovanni Bernardo Sessa, Fratelli, 1597.

4°, 4 + 375 + 1 ff., 220 x 160, print field 172 x 115, 37 lines per page, red and black ink. The *Compendium* appears on folios 319v to 328r.

Mansell 99, 554; Bohatta II, # 391.

Copy consulted: Newberry Library, Chicago.

Three other imprints were not available during the preparation of this edition. Information about the following titles therefore derives only from secondary sources, but it is possible that the books exist somewhere. The physical descriptions are inconsistent because they are taken from secondary sources. It is doubtful that the *Familiaris Clericorum* below contains the *Compendium musices,* since most books with that title do not include the treatise. (See p. 28 below.) However, the two Sacerdotales listed probably raise the number of identifiable editions from 27 to 29.

Familiaris Clericorum Liber. Venice, Vittore Dei Ravani e Compagni, 1535.

8°, 8 + 242 ff., 36 lines per page.
Sander # 2650, but no location given.

[Title apparently matches R576.] Venice, Giunta, 1579.

4°, 4 + 375 ff. + 1.
Camerini pt. II, 88.[8]

[Title apparently matches R576]. Venice, Giovanni Battista Sessa [il Giovane] e Fratelli, 1585.[9]

4°, 375 ff., 215 x 160.
Ales, p. 277–278; BM *GenCat* 139, col. 508; Pancini, p. 138; Bohatta II, # 390.

[8] Camerini's physical description, although not detailed, is enough to suggest that this edition, like several others in the late sixteenth century, followed exactly the format represented by R576. Camerini provides no modern location.

[9] The citiations give two modern locations for this book. However, the British Library copy could not be found, and the staff suggests that it was destroyed during World War II; a copy reported at Santa Maria della Consolazione, Venice, was inaccessible because the librarian was hospitalized during my visit of May, 1981.

References to four other possible editions should probably be dismissed as mistakes. Mansell 99, 554, lists a *Sacerdotale,* printed at Venice by Giorgio dei Rusconi in 1510, among the holdings at the University of North Carolina, but this book seems to be a phantom.[10] RISM-Ecr II, 926, reports two surviving copies of a *Cantorinus* (Pietro Liechtenstein, 1541), but both of those prove to be copies of C549.[11] Similarly elusive is a Venetian *Cantorinus* (Eredi Pietro Dei Ravani, 1548), reported in RISM-Ecr II, 926, to survive only at the Biblioteca Nazionale Marciana, Venice.[12] Finally, Åke Davidssohn[13] lists a *Cantorinus* published by Giunta in 1530 at the Biblioteca del Conservatorio di Musica Santa Cecilia in Rome; no other indication of such a book is known, for the two editions now owned by that library are C513 and C549.[14]

Some other imprints invite confusion with editions listed above, but they do not contain the *Compendium.* Three such books can be classed as a Cantorinus; the colophon of the following 1523 and 1535 editions reveals the Benedictine nature of the book, "Cantorinus & processionarius . . . secundum ritum congregationis cassinensis alias sancte Iustine." These three books, already the subject of some atten-

[10] I am indebted to Professor Thomas Warburton, who visited the libraries at Chapel Hill on my behalf. A letter from Ms. Debra Skaradzinski (24 June, 1981), Reading Room Supervisor of the Rare Book Collection, reported that she, like me, could not confirm that such a book ever existed.

[11] The volume at Glasgow University possesses a torn title page with its date now gone; the colophon identifies the book as C549. As for the other copy, Dr. Watkins Shaw, Honorary Librarian of St. Michael's College, Tenbury Wells, Great Britain, wrote (personal letter, 1 July, 1981) that their book was also C549; this information corresponded to what he had provided earlier for the entries in RISM-Ecr.

[12] During May, 1981, librarians there joined me in a patient search through their catalogues, including a handwritten checklist of editions from the Ravani house. We could not confirm that such an edition ever existed.

[13] Åke Davidssohn, *Bibliographie der Musiktheoretischen Drücke des 16. Jahrhunderts,* in *Biblioteca Bibliographica Aureliana* IX (1962), 20.

[14] For this information I am indebted to Jeffrey Dean, who visited the library on my behalf.

tion by Giulio Cattin,[15] can be identified by these short titles:

Monastici cantus compendiolum . . . Venice, Lucantonio Giunta, 1506.
Cantus monastici formula noviter impressa . . . Venice, Lucantonio Giunta, 1523.
Cantus monastici formula nouiter impressa . . . Venice, Lucantonio Giunta, 1535.

A more difficult problem rises from the title *Familiaris clericorum* . . ., for a sizeable number of Venetian Rituales employed that title. Most of these books began with a brief essay on solmisation, but did not include the *Compendium.* Here is a chronological list of those short titles:

Familiaris Clericorum. Gregorio Dei Gregorio, Venice, 1517.
Copy consulted: Biblioteca Colombina, Seville.
Familiaris Clericorum libellus musices divinique cultus . . . Venice, Gregorio dei Gregorio, 1525.
Copy consulted: Biblioteca Apostolica Vaticana.
Familiaris Clericorum Liber Nuperrime ad proptatum commodum . . . Venice, Vittore dei Ravani e Compagni, 1540.
Copy consulted: Biblioteca Apostolica Vaticana.
Familiaris Clericorum Liber Nuperrime ad proptatum commodum . . . Venice, Pietro Liechtenstein, 1541.
Copy consulted: Biblioteca Apostolica Vaticana.
Familiaris Clericorum post omnes omnium impressiones . . . Venice, Eredi Lucantonio Giunta, 1542.
Copy consulted: Newberry Library, Chicago.
Familiaris Clericorum Liber Nuperrime ad proptatum commodum . . . Venice, Pietro Ravani e Compagni, 1549.
Copy consulted: Biblioteca Comunale dell'Archiginnasio, Bologna.

[15] Giulio Cattin, "Tradizione e tendenze innovatrici nella normativa e nella pratica liturgico-musicale della Congregazione di S. Giustina," *Benedictina* 17 (1970), 254–299.

[*Familiaris Clericorum*]. Venice, Eredi Pietro Liechtenstein, 1550.

Copy consulted: British Library, London.[16]

Familiaris Clericorum liber: iuxta antiquiorem formam . . . Venice, Giovanni Varisco e Compagni, 1560.[17]

Copy consulted: Civico Museo Bibliografico Musicale, Bologna.

Familiaris Clericorum liber: iuxta antiquiorem formam . . . Venice, Francesco Bindoni, 1561.

Copy consulted: Biblioteca Apostolica Vaticana.

Familiaris Clericorum liber iuxta antiquiorem formam . . . Venice, Giovanni Varisco e Compagni, 1565.

Copy consulted: Biblioteca Communale dell'Archiginnasio, Bologna.

16 The title page was lost from this copy, but the colophon identifies the printer and year of printing.

17 *A Liber Familiaris* at the Biblioteca Apostolica Vaticana possesses an incomplete title page, and it was catalogued there as possibly by *Ravani in 1550.* However, its physical characteristics match Varisco's edition of 1560, and the final page also bears Varisco's emblem.

ORIGINS AND MODIFICATIONS OF THE TEXT

About two-thirds of the verbiage and all but two of the musical examples have been found in earlier writings, notably Ugolino of Orvieto's *Declaratio Musicae Disciplinae*[18] and the *Lucidarium Musicae Planae* by Marchetto of Padua.[19] Relationships to such earlier material are tabulated below; numberings for the *Compendium's* sentences and musical examples derive from the following modern edition. If the *Compendium's* version paraphrases part of the original, this is indicated by the phrase, "Adapted from . . ."

1: Adapted from *Lucidarium, Tractatus* VIII, *Capitulum* IV, 2.

2–5: Adapted from *Declaratio* XV, 3–6.

6–8: *Lucidarium, Tractatus* XIV, 5–8.

9–16: Common-knowledge verses.[20]

17–18: Departs from *Declaratio* XI, 3–4, which includes gamma, thereby describing a gamut of 21 notes and 8 letters.

19–20: Adapted from *Declaratio* VII, 3–4.

21–27: Adapted from *Lucidarium, Tractatus* XIX, 12–15, 17–18.

40–47: A standard account of the seven *deductiones,*[21] but the exact source is not yet located.

48: Caption, *Declaratio* XVIII; sentence 48, *Declaratio* XVI, 8.

49: *Lucidarium, Tractatus* VIII, *Capitulum* II, 3.

52–55: *Declaratio* XVIII, 2–5.

Exx. 1–26: *Declaratio* XVII.

61–63 and caption: *Lucidarium, Tractatus* IX, 1–2, 6–7.

[18] Edited in Albert Seay, *Vgolini Vrbevatanis: Declaratio Musicae Disciplinae*, in *Corpus Scriptorum de Musica* 7 (1959).

[19] Edited in Jan Herlinger, *The "Lucidarium" of Marchetto of Padova: a Critical Edition, Translation, and Commentary* (Ph. D. dissertation, University of Chicago, 1978), 2 vols.

[20] For lists of writings quoting these, see Michel Huglo, *Les Tonaires, Inventaire, Analyse, Comparison* (Paris, 1971), p. 425; Wilfried Kaiser, *Dietrich Tzwyvel und sein Musiktractat* (Marburg, 1968), *Marburger Beiträge zur Musikforschung* II, 261; and William Waite, "Two Musical Poems of the Middle Ages," *Musik und Geschichte: Leo Schrade zum sechzigsten Geburtstag* (Köln, 1963), p. 28.

[21] See Oliver Ellsworth, " "The Origins of the Coniuncta: a Reappraisal," *Journal of Music Theory* 17 (1973), 88–89.

69–70: Adapted from *Declaratio* XX, 2–3 and 6.

Exx. 27–29: *Declaratio* XX (Greek vocabulary omitted in the *Compendium).*

72–75: A simplifying departure from *Declaratio* XXI.

Exx. 32, 33, 35: *Declaratio* XXI.

76–78 and Exx. 36–38: *Declaratio* XXII, 4, 7–8.

79–82 and Exx. 39–41: Adapted from *Declaratio* XXIII, 4, 13, 15–16.

83–84: Common-knowledge definitions, perhaps adapted from *Lucidarium, Tractatus* III, *Capitulum* I, 5–6.

Exx. 42–44: *Declaratio* XXV.

91–92: Common-knowledge definitions, perhaps adapted from *Lucidarium, Tractatus* III, *Capitulum* II, 2–3.

Exx. 45–48: *Declaratio* XXIX.

98–99: Common-knowledge definitions, perhaps adapted from *Lucidarium, Tractatus* III, *Capitulum* III, 2–3.

101: Perhaps condensed from *Declaratio* XXXVI, 16–22.

102: Preceding caption from *Declaratio* L, 1.

102–109: Adapted from *Declaratio* L, 19; LI, 3, 5–9; LII, 6.

111–115: Adapted from *Declaratio* LIII, 2, 11; LIV, 8–10.

Exx. 49–50: *Declaratio* LXI.

116–120: *Declaratio* LV, 2–3, 10; LVI, 2, 9.

Exx. 51–52: *Declaratio* LXI.

121–126: *Declaratio* LVII, 2–3, 11; LVIII, 2–4, 9.

Exx. 53–54: *Declaratio* LXI.

127–133: *Declaratio* LIX, 2–4, 10; LX, 2–4, 8.

Exx. 55–56: *Declaratio* LXI.

134–137: *Declaratio* LXI, 8–9; LXII, 5–6.

Exx. 57–64: *Declaratio* LXII.

138–140 and Exx. 65–66: *Declaratio* LXIII, 7–9.

141–144 and Exx. 67–68: *Declaratio* LXIII, 9–12.

145: *Declaratio* LXIII, 13.

147–150: See 9–16 above.

151: *Lucidarium, Tractatus* XII, 14.

152–154: *Lucidarium, Tractatus* XXII, 15–22, shortened and

paraphrased.

Consistent with the rather free editorial attitude evident in the original compilation, later editions were also prepared by people who departed from their models. Sometimes the editors inherited misprints which they corrected. (Some of those errors could be detected only by analyzing the grammar, which suggests that some editors took their tasks seriously.) Usually they made changes intended to save space or to clarify or expand the text. Printers were responding to the demands of the marketplace, and so they sought the most commercially successful version, not an historically authentic version. Following is a summary of the major changes in the text.

The first revision occurred in C513, which moved sentences 1–8 from the palm of the Guidonian hand to the beginning of the text proper. The eight verses concerning psalm tones were then moved from the very end of the treatise to 9–16, and the illustration of the gamut was added. (Plate II.) Apparently this editor was persuaded that the discussion of modes allowed some chants to resist classification, for he inserted a paraphrase from Marchetto at the very end, sentences 151–159. He then concluded by adding the reference to writings by St. Birgitta of Sweden (1303–1374). This version of the *Compendium* is the longest one known to survive, and it was followed by various later editors.

Evidently the editor of C550 needed to save space, for he deleted sentences 30–36, 50, 52–55, 60, the illustration of the gamut, the first 19 musical examples, and everything from 102 to the end. Therefore no discussion of modes obtains, and the editor may have recognized that the presentation of mutation was badly maimed, for he added after sentence 59, "Learn these mutations from the master teaching you."

A later edition, R564, reinstated the last third of the treatise (the discussion of modes) and the illustration of the gamut. Someone also rewrote the bothersome section on mutation (sentences 52–60) so that two musical examples were used. This editor also gave the 8 verses about psalm tones only at the end of the treatise (after sentence 146) and moved sentences 1–8 to after sentence 38. Furthermore, the editor of R564 inherited an inconsistency which appears not to have troubled earlier editors. Although the treatise provides no distinction between major and minor semitones, those two terms are used several times. Most of the problematic adjectives, *minus* and *maius,* are deleted in R564. The changes in this edition seem to have been well received, for they were endorsed by numerous later editions.

One final revision of interest is the effort of R587 and R588 to clarify organization by adding consistent, numbered chapter titles throughout the treatise.

EDITORIAL PROCEDURES

This is a critical edition in the full sense, for the presented text reflects many personal judgments. My first principle has been to follow recent editorial trends favoring the readability of a "clear text,"[22] limiting editorial intrusions as much as possible. Sentences and musical examples are numbered, but the editorial apparatus appears as endnotes rather than as footnotes.

Since fidelity to text models was an anachronistic concept in the history of the *Compendium,* arguments could favor trying to portray the changing nature of this material. If, however, the text is to reflect the flow of an original, it can be only one version, with alternatives delegated to unequal status, the critical apparatus. The printing of 1513 is the one chosen here because it is the first edition to provide the most complete version. The following edition observes the organization of C513 and prefers its readings, but if earlier sources offer more correct details, C513's version is recorded in the Critical Notes.

The numerous editions contain a myriad of minor differences; to record all those details in the Critical Notes would go far beyond the patience of most readers. Capitalization, punctuation, abbreviations, and spelling have been modernized without notifying the reader. The following other details have also been expunged from the apparatus:

1. Most obvious misprints, as well as disagreements between B and #. (The exceptions here are mistaken solmisation syllables and letter names for pitches; these disagreements, although small, alter meanings significantly.)
2. Variants in neume forms.
3. Contrasting formats for the captions of musical examples.
4. Variants involving the words *videlicet* and *scilicet.*

This is not to imply that information about accidentals is without value, but that most readers do not require such information. Other disagreements between sources, more substantive ones, are listed in the Critical

[22] Thomas Tanselle, "Some Principles for Editorial Apparatus," *Studies in Bibliography* 25 (1972), 45.

Notes. Sometimes the *Compendium's* quotations of earlier sources are faulty. If the error is a brief omission, the missing material is supplied in parentheses; more complex matters are reported in the Critical Notes.

Seeking to give the Critical Notes a less awkward design, and also to make a clear grouping of editions sharing a given variant, a method of concatenating consecutive editions is used. For example, "R537–88" refers to all Rituales printed from 1537 to 1588, but not to editions of the *Cantorinus* appearing during the same years. The Critical Notes employ the following scheme for pitch registers:

C–B c–b c'–b' c"–b"

THE GUIDONIAN HAND

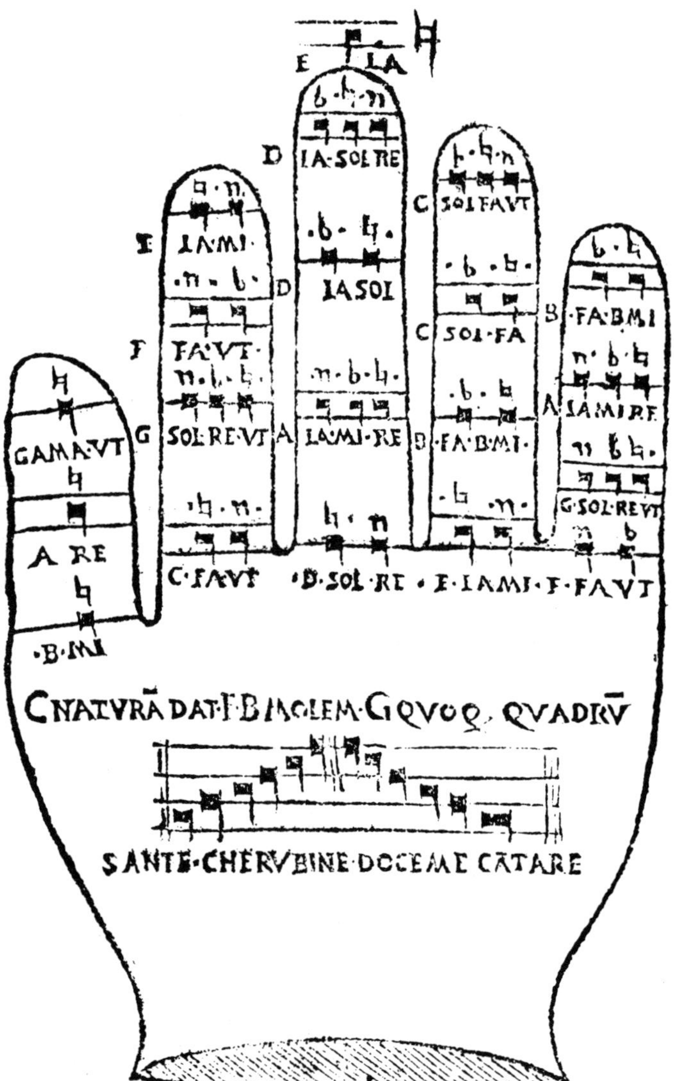

THE GAMUT

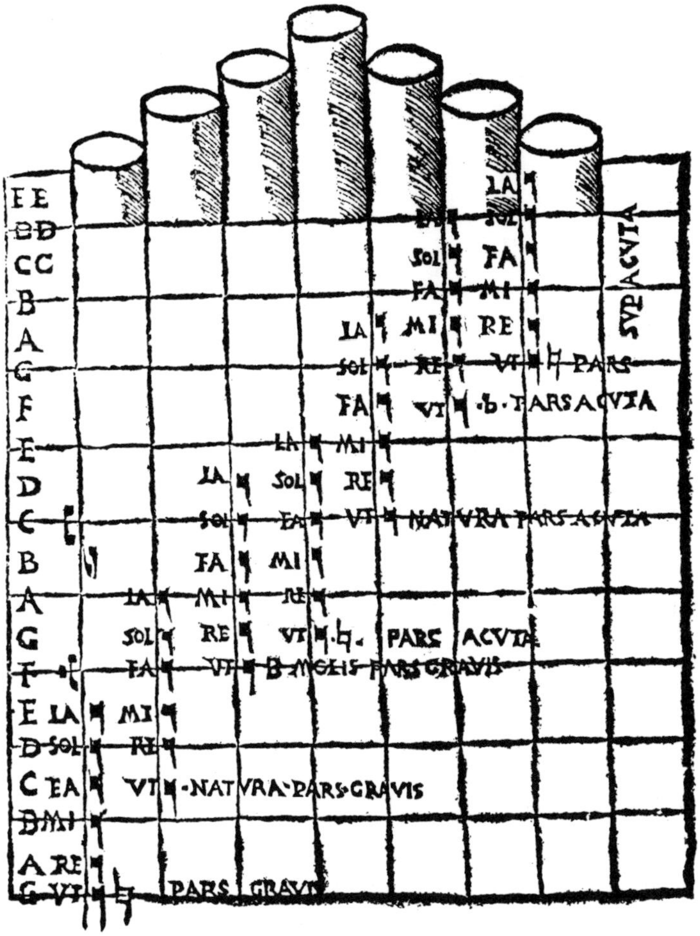
SUPACUTA
PARS ACUTA
NATURA PARS ACUTA
PARS ACUTA
NATURA PARS GRAVIS
PARS GRAVIS

COMPENDIUM MUSICES

[See Plate I]

[1]Proprietas in musica est derivatio plurium vocum, ab uno eodemque principio. [2]Existentibus igitur modis sive proprietatibus tribus totius cantus, pro ipsarum habenda notitia, cuilibet unica est littera assignata. [3]Nam proprietati naturae data est littera C, B molli F, et # quadro G, quibus vocum principium proprietatum conceditur, scilicet, ut vox, quam ceterae sibi ordinatae voces, videlicet, re mi fa sol la per eandem proprietatem sequuntur; ut enim vox in C locata cum suis ordinatis vocibus, scilicet, re mi fa sol la per proprietatem naturae in gravi vel acuto cantatur. [4]In F per B molle, in G per # quadrum, unde versus:

[5]Naturae modum per C cantare solemus,
F B molle notat, sed G quadrum ostendit.

[6]Nota quod signa sive claves, ut vulgo dicitur, demonstrantes sedem totius cantus universaliter usitatae sunt duae, videlicet F grave, loco cuius litterae talis figura ponitur et C acutum, pro quo fit tale signum. .[7]Per ipsarum autem discretam repositionem per lineas potest omnis cantus cuiuscunque sit toni rationabiliter collocari. [8]Distant enim abinvicem per diapente, nam F in gravibus, C in acutis constituta sunt.

Versus

[9]Re la vult primus, re fa retinetque secundus,
[10] Per sextam mi fa terno, quarto dato mi la,
[11]Fa fa fert quintus, fa la praebet tibi sextus,
[12]Ut sol septenus, ut fa captatque supremus.

De intonatione psalmorum dantur hi versus, videlicet,

[13]Primus cum sexto, fa sol la semper habeto,
[14]Tertius et octavus, ut re fa, atque secundus,

[15] La sol la quartus, ut mi sol sit tibi quintus,
[16] Septimus fa mi fa sol, sic omnes esse recordor.

[See Plate II]

[17] Quisquis ad canendi scientiam erudiendus accedis, dispositionem, vim, et ordinem, litterarum, per quas omnis cantus habet discretionem, cordi memoriter inprimas, videlicet quod ponuntur et sunt in ordine manus seu palmae viginti litterae, quae dividuntur in subgravibus, gravibus, acutis, et superacutis. [18] At vero ipsae litterae in ordine manus non sunt nisi septem, voce et forma differentes, scilicet, A, #, C, D, E, F, G. [19] Subgravis una est duntaxat littera Graeca omnium prima in principio pollicis manus sinistrae a Latinis philosophis addita, quam quidam eorum vocabulo Gamma dicunt, nos vero Latini G appellamus. [20] In qua nostrae musicae omnis sumit ordo principium et ipsius gamma nostra manus ornata initio se a Graecis profitetur exordium assumpsisse. [21] Graves litterae sunt septem, scilicet, A, #, C, D, E, F, G, et graves dicuntur, quia in inferiori loco primitus sunt formatae, hoc est in voce pectoris. [22] Habentque principium in prima iunctura pollicis, et finem in secunda iunctura auricularis. [23] Acutae similiter sunt septem, scilicet, a, # c, d, e, f, g, quae non sunt a primis gravibus nomine differentes, sed forma dumtaxat. [24] Ideoque acutae dicuntur, eo quod acutum reddant sonum respectum gravium praedicatorum. [25] Formantur enim in superiori loco, id est in voce gutturis et habent principium in tertia iunctura auricularis, finem vero in secunda iunctura indicis. [26] Superacutae sunt quinque, scilicet, aa, ##, cc, dd, ee, et ideo superacutae dicuntur eo quod super praedictas acutas acutiorem reddant sonum. [27] Et ratio est quia formantur in superiori loco, scilicet in voce capitis, et habent principium in secunda iunctura medii, finem vero in tertia iunctura eiusdem a tergo, ut omni depictam hanc manum intuenti patet.

[28] Ut autem ordo litterarum naturaliter positarum ibi breviter pateat, et quae in spatio, quae vel litterae sint in linea cognoscas,

inferius perpende dispositas Gamma in linea A in spatio, # in linea, C in spatio, D in linea, E in spatio, F in linea, G in spatio, a in linea, # in spatio, c in linea, d in spatio, e in linea, f in spatio, g in linea, aa in spatio, ## in linea, cc in spatio, dd in linea, ee in spatio. [29] Vide quia litterae quae in gravibus in linea notantur, in acutis in spatio demonstrantur, et quae in acutis in spatio sunt notatae, in superacutis in linea sunt scriptae.

[30] Praeterea sciendum est quod B rotundum in dispositione litterarum non debet proprie lineam aut spatium occupare nec locum naturaliter habere, quia non est de computo septem litterarum musicalium; si enim esset aliqua de septem, per duplarem consonantiam alicui gravium vel superacutarum responderet. [31] Gravibus quippe per duplarem respondere non potest consonantiam, quia minus esset semitonium. [32] Superacutis vero per diapason nequaquam consonat, quia semitonium superabundat. [33] Vocatur enim apud Graecos B rotundum sive menon, hoc est accidens vel accidentale, quod enim est accidentale non est proprium, et quod non est proprium non est naturale. [34] Inventum est autem B rotundum ad temperandum tritonum, qui super scilicet naturaliter inventitur; ubi enim cantus asperior sonat, B rotundum loco # quadri ad temperandam tritoni duritiam furtim interponitur. [35] Sed ubi cantus ad suam naturam recurrerit, statim debet auferri. [36] Igitur quia B rotundum est accidens vel accidentale, et accidens potest adesse vel abesse sine corruptione subiecti, ubi necessarium fuerit apponatur. [37] Nec id te lateat quod praedictis septem litteris voce et forma differentibus associate sunt notulae seu voces sex, scilicet, ut re mi fa sol la quae ex duabus primis proprietatibus, scilicet # quadri, et naturae quinquies repetitae ponuntur, et ex tertia scilicet, B rotundi proprietate bis interponi noscuntur. [38] Sunt ergo notae omnes in manu numero quadraginta duae numeratae, videlicet a gamma ad ee ultimum viginti sedibus collocatae. [39] Et nota quod syllaba ut semper est caput et principium aliarum sibi succedentium syllabarum, scilicet, re mi fa sol la. [40] Harum enim omnium sex syllabarum aggregatio dicitur in cantu deductio, quia deducit modulantium voces ex gravitate in acumen, et ex acumine in gravitatem. [41] Et quia illa nota sive syllaba, ut, septies in

manu reperitur, ideo dicimus quod septem sunt deductiones manus seu palmae, unde prima deductio habet principium in G subgravi, et finem in E gravi, et cantatur per # quadrum grave. [42] Secunda habet principium in C gravi, et finem in a acuto, et cantatur per naturam gravem. [43] Tertia habet principium in F gravi, finem vero in d acuto, et cantatur per B molle grave. [44] Quarta habet principium in G gravi, et finem in e acuto, et cantatur per # quadrum acutum. [45] Quinta habet principium in c acuto, finem vero in aa superacuto, et cantatur per naturam acutam. [46] Sexta habet principium in f acuto, et finem in dd superacuto, et cantatur per B molle acutum. [47] Septima habet principium in g acuto, finem vero in ee superacuto, et cantatur per ## quadrum superacutum.

Brevis et utilis regula pro fiendis mutationibus

[48] Mutatio est alicuius vocis vel notae unius proprietatis in alteram eiusdem soni atque loci varietatae acceptio. [49] Fit namque mutatio vel fieri potest in quolibet loco ubi duae vel tres voces sive notae nomine sunt diversae, quae suidem sub una sola littera includuntur. [50] Itaque ad mutationem faciendam requiritur quod ibi sint duae voces unisonum facientes, et quod proprietates per quas sit mutatio iungantur ad invicem in una voce. [51] Unde ubi sola vox est, non potest fieri mutatio; etiam si sint duae voces et non sint aequales in sono, non fit mutatio, ut sunt illae duae voces de B fa # mi, quae differunt sono per semitonium maius, quod est inter fa et mi. [52] Praeterea notare debemus vocum variandarum finem, quarum si terminatio fiat in ut vel in re vel in mi tunc ascendendo facimus mutationem. [53] Si vero vocum variandarum terminatio sit in fa vel in sol vel in la tunc descendendo mutamus. [54] Patent ista in subscriptis mutationum exemplis ubi ut re mi ad invicem variamus quia tunc semper ascendendo mutamus fa sol la semper descendendo variamus, unde versus:

[55] Ut re mi scandimus si variare volemus,
Sed descendemus si fa sol la variamus.

[56] Item nota quod non debet fieri mutatio nisi necessiate cogente,

unde duplex est necessitas. [57]Prima est quando proprietas una non sufficit ad ascensum vel descensum cantus, et tunc oportet mutationem fieri proprietatis ipsius in aliam cantui magis deservientem. [58]Et quandiu per unam proprietatem potest cantari, non debet fieri alterius proprietatis mutatio, sed vitari. [59]Secunda necessitas est, quod licet una proprietas per ascensum vel descensum cantui deserviret, tamen de necessitate mutatur in aliam ad cantum magis armonicum faciendum, ut saepe fit de B molle in # duro et econverso, et tunc totaliter non debet vitari mutatio.

Primus mutationis locus # quadri et naturae [Ex.1]

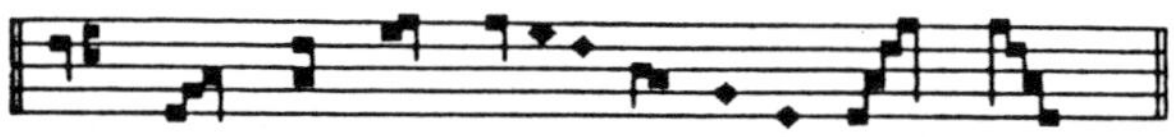

C grave et primum

Secundus mutationis locus # quadri et naturae [Ex. 2]

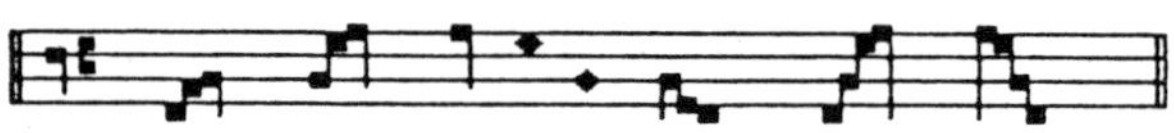

D grave et primum

Tertius mutationis locus # quadri et naturae [Ex. 3]

E grave et primum

Quartus mutationis locus naturae et B mollis [Ex. 4]

F grave et primum

Quintus mutationis locus [Exx. 5–6]

Locus naturae et B mollis — Locus naturae et # quadri

G acutum et secundum — G acutum et secundum

Quintus mutationis locus [Ex. 7]
Locus B mollis et # quadri

Sextus mutationis locus [Ex. 8]
Locus naturae et B mollis

G acutum et secundum — a acutum et secundum

Sextus mutationis locus [Exx. 9–10]

Locus naturae et # quadri — Locus B mollis et # quadri

a acutum et secundum — a acutum et secundum

Septimus mutationis locus [Exx. 11–12]

Locus B mollis et # quadri — Locus B mollis et naturae acutae

c acutum et secundum — c acutum et secundum

Septimus mutationis locus # quadri et naturae acutae [Ex. 13]

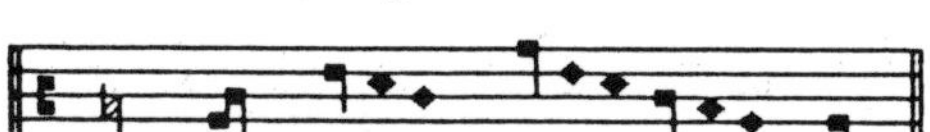

c acutum et secundum

Octavus mutationis locus B mollis et # quadri [Ex. 14]

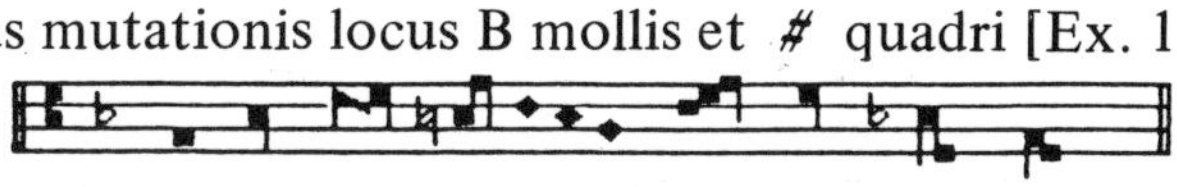

d acutum et secundum

Octavus mutationis locus [Exx. 15–16]

Locus B mollis et naturae | Locus # quadri et naturae acutae

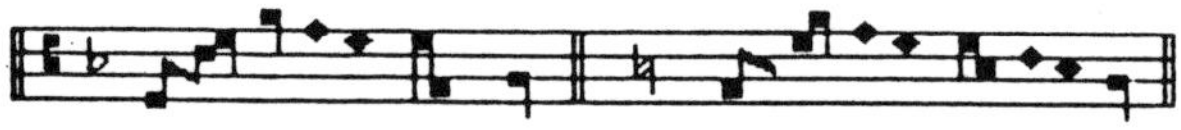

d acutum et secundum | d acutum et secundum

Nonus mutationis locus # quadri et naturae acutae [Ex. 17]

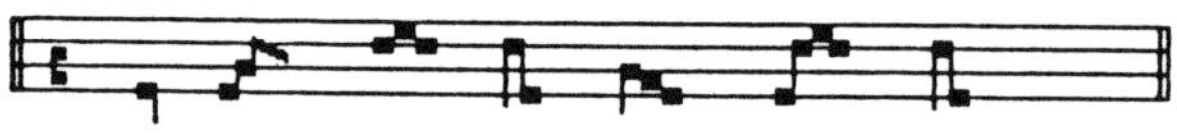

e acutum et secundum

Decimus mutationis locus naturae et B mollis [Ex. 18]

f acutum et secundum

Undecimus mutationis locus [Exx. 19–20]

Locus naturae acutae et B mollis acutae | Locus naturae acutae et # quadri superacutae

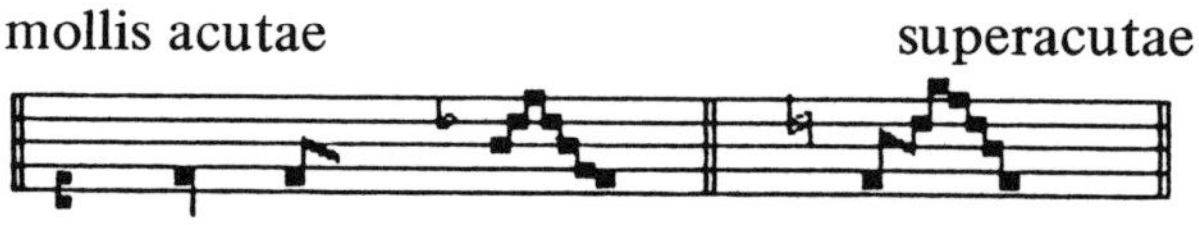

g superacutum et tertium | g superacutum et tertium

Undecimus mutationis locus [Ex. 21]

Locus B mollis et # quadri

g superacutum et tertium

Duodecimus mutationis locus [Exx. 22–23]

Locus naturae acutae et B mollis

Locus naturae et # quadri superacutae

aa superacutum et tertium

aa superacutum et tertium

Duodecimus mutationis locus B mollis et # quadri superacutae [Ex. 24]

aa superacutum et tertium

Tertiusdecimus mutationis locus [Ex. 25]

cc superacutum et tertium

Quartusdecimus mutationis locus [Ex. 26]

dd superacutum et tertium

60 Notato ordine litterarum per lineas et spatia positarum ac vocum deductionibus, ad dispositionem coniunctionum et consonantiarum

veniamus.

De coniunctionibus vocum quid sint (et quot)

[61]Coniunctio in musica est disposito sive ordinatio sonorum sive vocum ad invicem in syllabis et dictionibus. [62]Tonus igitur semitonium, ditonus et semiditonus coniunctiones vocantur quae consonantiarum membra proprie nuncupantur. [63]Unde Isidorus: toni, semitonia, ditoni, semiditoni, sunt particulae consonantiarum per quas voces vocibus et cantibus cantus iunguntur. [64]Tonus a tono non differt in aliquo, nec semitonium a semitonio, similiter autem ditonus a ditono non nullo modo discrepat, nec semiditonus a semiditono. [65]Licet enim tonus, semitonium, ditonus, semiditonus pluribus in locis in manu reperiantur, idem tamen semper sunt quod superius esse diffiniuntur. [66] Quisquis igitur bene, naturaliter, et perfecte cantare desideras, habeas coniunctiones per manus articulos determinatas. [67]Insuper si menti memoriter insertas cum adiunctis consonantiis tenueris, peritus cantor si adsit possibilitas vocis facile esse poteris, quoniam quod ore decantes tentabis auditu et corde intelligere praevalebis. [68]Sed iam primo videamus quid sit tonus.

De tono

[69]Tonus (igitur), qui omnium prima et integra dicitur esse coniunctio, est duorum sonorum inaequalium per spatium integrum immediate iunctorum acceptio. [70]Dicitur autem tonus a tonando, id est perfecte et integre pronuntiando, quia utrumque sonum plene et integre pronuntiare debemus. [71] Et est tonus inter G et A et econverso, et ab A ad ♮ et econverso, inter C et D et econverso, et ab D ad E et econverso, et ab F ad g et econverso in gravibus, acutis, et superacutis, ut hic patet exemplo. [Exx. 27–31]

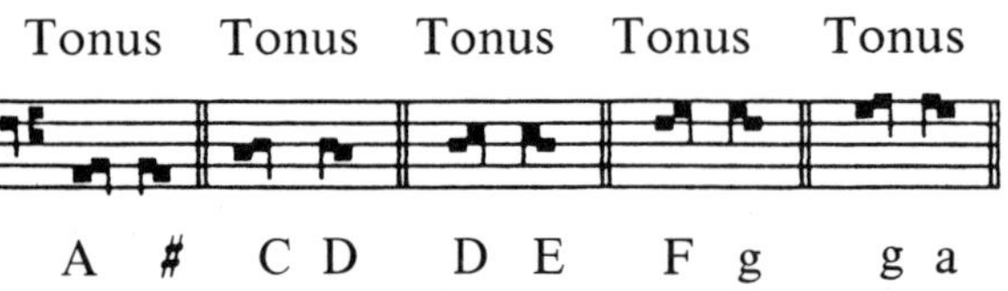

De semitonio

[72] Semitonium minus est duorum sonorum inaequalium per spatium imperfectum et non integrum immediate iunctorum acceptio. [73] Et dicitur semitonium a semi quod est imperfectum, vel incompletum, vel non integrum, et tonus quasi imperfectus et non integer tonus. [74] Et ideo sicut tonus perfecte, complete, et integre pronuntiatur, ita semitonium quod duarum partium toni minor pars est imperfecte, incomplete, et non integre pronuntiari debet, quod manifeste intelligentium prolatione et in monachordo patet. [75] Et est semitonium inter ♯ quadratum et C et econverso, E et F et econverso, A et B rotundum et econverso in gravibus, acutis, et superacutis, ut hic patet exemplo. [Exx. 32–35]

Semitonium Semitonium Semitonium Semitonium

♯ C E F a b ♯ c

De ditono

[76] Ditonus est duorum sonorum seu vocum per duo spatia plena, integra, atque perfecta, iunctorum acceptio. [77] Habet ergo ditonus duos tonos, voces tres et intervalla duo, et quia ex tonis est eius compositio debet esse perfecta, plena, et integra eius pronuntiatio. [78] Dicitur autem ditonus a dia quod est duo, et tonus quia ex duobus (con)-iungitur tonis, ut hic patet exemplo. [Exx. 36–38]

Ditonus Ditonus Ditonus

C E F a c e

[79] Semiditonus est trium vocum seu sonorum per spatium unum plenum, integrum, atque perfectum, et aliud non integrum, atque

imperfectum iunctorum acceptio. [80]Et dicitur semiditonus a semi quod est non plenum et non perfectum et ditonus quasi imperfectus tonus cum perfecto et completo tono. [81] Perfectam quippe habere non potest semiditonus pronuntiationem sicut ditonus, quia ex maioris semitonii deperditione ad ditoni perfecta spatia non attingit. [82]Idcirco toni perfectam et semitonii imperfectam habent prolationem, ut hic sequitur. [Exx. 39–41]

Semiditonus Semiditonus Semiditonus

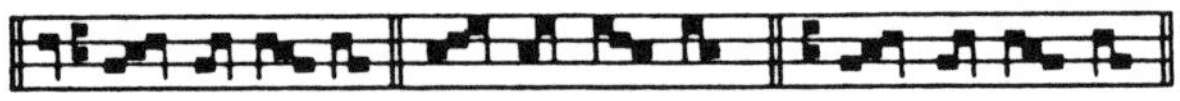

D F E G a c

De diatessaron Prima consonantia

[83]Diatessaron consonantia fit ex quattuor sonis constituentibus duos tonos et unum semitonium minus. [84]Dicta est enim a dia quod est de et tessaron quattuor, quasi ex quattuor vocibus facta. [85]Igitur quoniam diatessaron consonantia quattuor retinet voces, tres tantum necesse est habeat differentes species. [86]Omnis namque consonantia unam semper minus habet speciem quam fuerint eius voces. [87]Prima namque eius species formatur ex tono, semitonio, et tono in elevatione. [88]Incipitur enim id est A re prima corda Graecorum, et procedit ad quartam litteram, scilicet, D his syllabis, re mi fa sol, et ubicumque reperiuntur similes voces, semper fit prima diatessaron species. [89]Secunda species diatessaron elevatur semitonio et duobus tonis incipiendo in ♮ mi, hisque quattuor syllabis procedit, mi fa sol la et ubicumque similis vocum commixtio reperitur, semper fit secunda species diatessaron. [90]Tertia vero species diatessaron elevatur duobus tonis et semitonio in formatione, incipiturque in C fa ut et procedit per has voces, ut re mi fa ac ubicumque reperitur similis vocum aggregatio, semper fit

tertia diatessaron species, ut hic patet inferius. [Exx. 42–44]

Prima species diatessaron | Secunda species diatessaron | Tertia species diatessaron

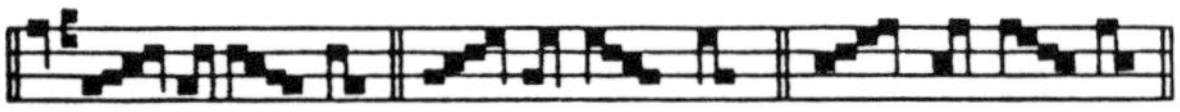

A D ♯ E C F

De Diapente Secunda consonantia

[91] Diapente est consonantia ex quinque sonis, tres tonos, unumque semitonium minus continentibus facta. [92] Dicta est enim a dia quod est de et penta quinque quasi consonantia ex quinque vocibus mixta. [93] Fit equidem diapente ex diatessaron et tono superaddito, quae cum quinque tantum habeat voces, quattuor necesse est retineat species. [94] Prima namque diapente species formatur ex prima specie diatessaron ex tono in acuto repente superadditio procedens his syllabis, re, mi, fa, sol, la, intensive, et ubicumque fuerit similium coniunctio vocum, semper fit prima species diapente. [95] Secunda species diapente formatur ex secunda specie diatessaron, ut supra procedit namque per has syllabas, mi, fa, sol, la, mi. [96] Tertia diapente species formatur ex tritono et semitono hisque procedit syllabis, fa, ut, re, mi, fa, et ubicumque fuerit similium connexio vocum, semper fit tertia species diapente. [97] Quarta vero species diapente formatur ex tertia specie diatessaron, et tono in acutiori parte superaddito procedens his syllabis, ut, re, mi, fa, sol, et ubicumque fuerit similium sonorum commixtio fit semper quarta species diapente, ut hoc monstratur exemplo. [Exx. 45–48]

Prima spiecies diapente | Secunda species diapente

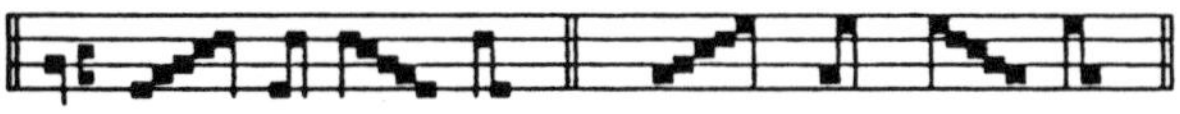

D a E ♯

Tertia species diapente Quarta species diapente

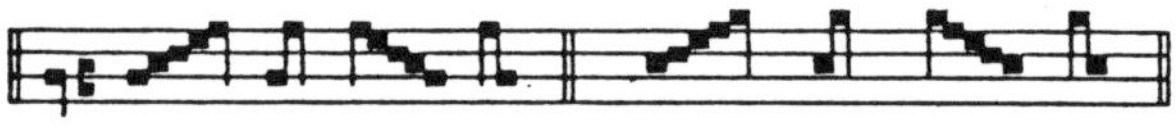

F c G d

De consonantia diapason

[98] Diapason consonantia fit ex octo sonis constituentibus quinque tonos et duo semitonia minora. [99] Dicitur enim a dia quod est de et pason omne, quasi consonantia consistens ex omnibus sonis. [100] Omnes quidem soni sunt septem in tota musicae disciplina, quibus cum primo replicato haec perfecta diapason simphonia perficitur. [101] Septem sunt differentes diapason species, quarum prima fit ab A gravi ad a acutum, secunda a # gravi ad # acutum, tertia a C gravi ad c acutum, quarta a D gravi ad d acutum, quinta ab E gravi ad e acutum, sexta ab F gravi ad f acutum, septima a G gravi ad g acutum.

De tropi seu toni descriptione

[102] Tropus, tonus sive modus est quam plurium vocum ex diapente ac diatessaron ordinationis speciebus debitae coniunctarum, in acumine et gravitate distantium, per ascensum et descensum congrua neumarum forma constitutarum, conveniens dispositio. [103] Et ideo Graeci, a quibus haec musica primitus est exorta, quattuor tropos, scilicet protum, deuterum, tritum, et tetrardum, sub quattuor vocum cognitione, scilicet, re, mi, fa, sol, ac D, E, F, G, primarum litterarum finalium terminatione statuere notandos, ut ex huiusmodi finalium litterarum atque vocum effectus notitia in ipsorum troporum perfectionis et naturae notitiam veniremus. [104] Protus namque tropus qui primus est in voce re et D prima sibi coniuncta littera cum suo subiugali finitur. [105] Deuterus qui secundus est tropus in mi voce et E prima littera cum suo subiugali finalem sedem acquirit. [106] Tritus vero qui tertius tropus est eiusque subiugalis in voce fa atque F prima (littera) est terminatus. [107] Sed tetrar-

dus tropus quartus in voce sol G quae prima cum suo subiugali est conflatus. [108] Hae quidem voces et litterae graves sunt, et in eis troporum termini statuuntur, ut autenticorum perfectionibus atque plagalium eorumque formationibus satisfiat. [109] Sunt ergo octo tropi sive toni numero differentes, quorum quilibet suam formam, ordinem atque modum habent, ut infra patebit.

[110] Quomodo praedicti tropi modi seu toni ex supra nominatis speciebus, scilicet, diatessaron, diapente, ac diapason constituantur ac formentur

[111] Protus tropus sive tonus qui in ordine primus est suam formam et esse a diapente et diatessaron recipit, quoniam ex ipsorum primis speciebus formatur, scilicet, re la prima diapente specie et ex re sol prima diatessaron, ipsi primae diapente superaddita speciei; producunt enim diapason hae coniunctae species quae sunt re la et re sol in D primo termino inferiori fundatae, et in D secundo termino superiori terminatae. [112] Forma igitur huius primi tropi seu toni autentici constat ex prima diapente specie, re la, et ex prima diatessaron superius adiuncta re sol, cuius formae demonstratio inferius patebit. [113] Forma subiugalis proti tropi sive toni est in D primo cum suo re prima diapente species inchoata, scilicet, re, la, et ab eiusdem prima diatessaron deorsum tendens species ordinata, scilicet, sol re. [114] Quae forma a sui autentici specierum auctoritate non deficit, quamquam in diatessaron positione ab autentici forma distet, utriusque tamen finis idem est. [115] Forma igitur plagalis huius est ex diapente specie prima, re la, et ex diatessaron etiam prima diapente ipsi cuniuncta inferius, sol re, ut inferius patet exemplo.[Exx. 49–50]

Demonstratio proti perfecti

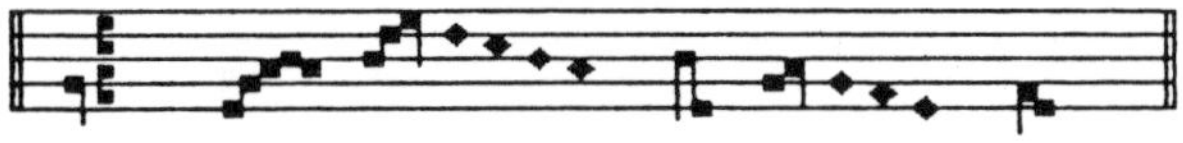

Diapason ex diapente et diatessaron connexa superius

Demonstratio plagalis proti perfecti

Diapason ex diapente et diatessaron connexa inferius

[116] Deuterus tropus seu tonus, qui autenticorum secundus sed in troporum ordine tertius est, ex diapente ac diatessaron recipit suam formam et esse. [117] Ex secunda enim diapente specie in E primo et voce sua mi inchoante et in secundo # et sua voce mi terminante ac etiam ex secunda diatessaron specie in eodem # cum voce sua mi initium habente et ad E secundum et suam vocem la terminante formatur. [118] Praesentis igitur tropi seu toni formatio ex mi mi specie diapente secunda et ex mi la etiam diatessaron secunda ipsi diapente superaddita speciei conficitur, ex quibus hic tropus redditur omnino perfectus, ut inferius patebit. [119] Forma subiugalis deuteri ab ipsius deuteri forma nisi in diatessaron positione non distat, quoniam ex (eiusdem et) diapente et diatessaron speciebus recipit suam formam et utriusque finis idem est. [120] Igitur haec forma in E primo suaque voce mi fundata ex secunda, ut diximus, specie componitur diapente ad # secundum eiusque mi vocem superius ascendente et ab eodem E atque voce cum coniuncta diapente ex secunda diatessaron specie descendente, quae forma est ex mi (mi) diapente secunda et ex la mi diatessaron inferius secunda specie, ut (hic) patet. [Exx. 51–52]

Demonstratio deuteri perfecti

Diapason ex diapente et diatessaron coniuncta superius

Demonstratio plagalis deuteri perfecti

Diapason ex diapente et diatessaron coniuncta inferius

[121]Tritus tropus sive tonus qui autenticorum tertius sed in troporum ordine quintus est ex diapente et diatessaron consonantiis suam formam acquirit et esse. [122]Nam forma haec in tertia diapente tertiaque diatessaron specie iunctis conficitur; ex eius namque fine atque fundamento, quod F primum dicitur, tertia diapente species exorta, scilicet, fa fa, in secunda, c terminata, cum coniuncta sibi specie tertia diatessaron, scilicet, ut fa, id est, ad secundum f, progressa finitur, quae ipsam diapason consonantiam perfectae constituunt. [123]Recta igitur forma triti ex fa fa tertia diapente et ut fa tertia diatessaron est coniuncta, ut (hic) patet inferius. [124]Forma subiugalis triti ex sui triti autentici speciebus, quoniam ipsius naturae est, acquirit esse et eius(dem) materiae cum ipso dicitur esse forma. [125]Verum quia, ut de ceteris dictum est plagalibus, diatessaron consonantia pro huismodi forma infra diapente coniungitur, quae pro autentici forma supra diapente connectitur, non videtur distare a ceteris, et utriusque idem est fundamentum et finis. [126]Huius igitur forma plagalis ex superius specie diapente tertia fit a fine fa fa et sub ipso coniuncta tertia diatessaron fa ut, ut patet hic inferius. [Exx. 53–54]

Demonstratio triti perfecti

Diapason ex diapente et diatessaron coniuncta superius

Demonstratio plagalis triti perfecti

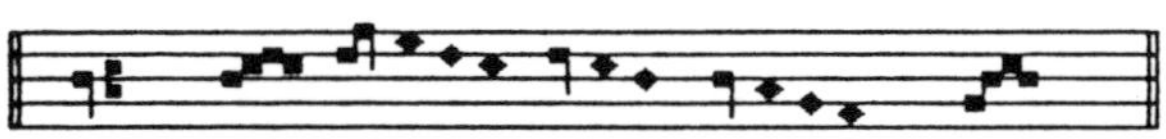

Diapason ex diapente et diatessaron coniuncta inferius

[127]Tetrardus tropus sive tonus autenticorum ultimus est qui in ordine tonorum septimus ex diapente ac diatessaron tamquam ex causis efficientibus suam formam et esse accipit et acquirit. [128] Omnes namque tropos eae consonantiae suis speciebus efficiunt, ut clare constat ex

supradictis. [129] Hanc etenim tetrardi formam quarta species diapente producit quae in G primo fundata ad D secundum cum ut sol terminanda producitur, et ab eodem D cum prima diatessaron re sol ad G secundum ulterius procedendo finitur. [130] Et ideo in eo G primo ut sol quarta diapente fundata cum re sol diatessaron prima coniuncta, huius tetrardi tropi dicitur esse forma, et perfectio, ut inferius constat exemplo. [131] Forma plagalis tetrardi, qui in ordine omnium ultimus et octavus est, a forma ipsius autentici tetrardi sumitur qui a quarta diapente et a prima diatessaron speciebus formatur. [132] Sola quippe diatessaron speciei (dis)posito inter eos differentiam facit, quae in autentico supra diapente componitur, sed in hoc plagali supponitur ut in ceteris plagalibus lex ista servatur G quoque primum utriusque fundamentum et finis est. [133] Istius igitur plagalis forma ex diapente specie quarta supra et ex diatessaron prima componitur infra, scilicet, ut sol, et sol re, ut inferius patet exemplo. [Exx. 55–56]

Demonstratio tetrardi perfecti

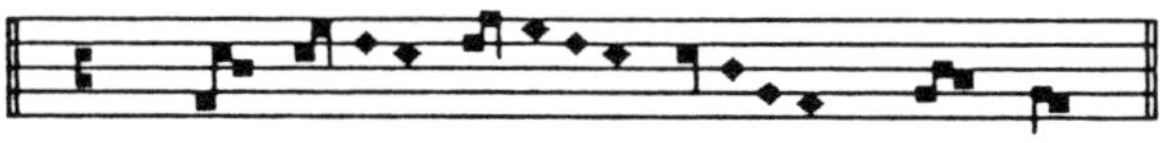

Diapason ex diapente cui adiungitur superius diatessaron

Demonstratio plagalis tetrardi perfecti

Diapason ex diapente cui infra adiungitur diatessaron

[134] Potest igitur perfectus tonus seu tropus tali declaratione describi: [135] Tropus seu tonus perfectus autenticus sive plagalis est qui ex ordinatis ex diapente ac diatessaron speciebus in acumine et gravitate coniunctis, debita neumarum posita dispositione rite diapason retinet perfectam formam. [136] Illa igitur ascensu contrario erit imperfectio tropi quae diapason perfectam formam non retinebit, perfectam diapason formam non retinere est a totali eius ascensu deficere, et ideo ille tropus nuncupabitur imperfectus, si autenticus est, qui a fine suo in dicto diapason

ascensu deficiet, ut si ad quintam, sextam vel septimam tantum attingit a fine, et tanto magis est imperfectus quanto magis a perfecta diapason distat. [137] Plagalis autem iudicabitur imperfectus, si a fine supra a diapente deficiat vel infra si diatessaron non descendat et in ea est imperfectus parte in qua deficiens invenitur et si in utraque deficiat, in utraque continet imperfectionem et dicitur in utraque imperfectus, ut patet exemplo.

Demonstratio proti imperfecti [Ex. 57]

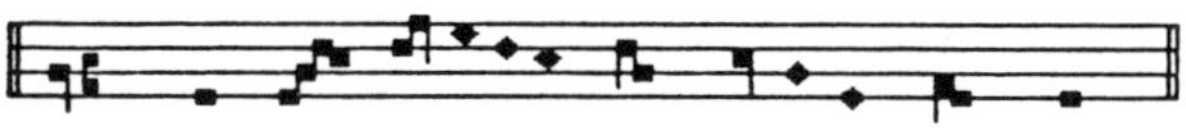

Diapason ex tono deficiens superioris toni continet imperfectionem

Demonstratio plagalis proti imperfecti [Ex. 58]

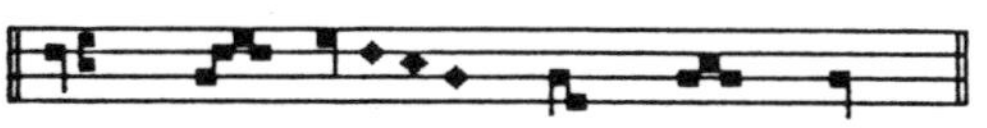

Diapason in utroque termino tono deficiens;
plagalem imperfectum reddit

Demonstratio deuteri imperfecti [Ex. 59]

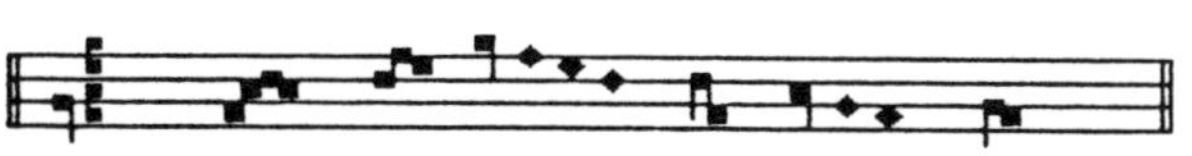

Diapason qui in tono superius deficit tropum imperfectum reddit

Demonstratio plagalis deuteri imperfecti [Ex. 60]

Diapason a # primo ad secundum est in tono inferiori deficiens

Demonstratio triti imperfecti [Ex. 61]

Diapason in inferiori tono deficiens; tropi continet imperfectionem

Demonstratio plagalis triti imperfecti [Ex. 62]

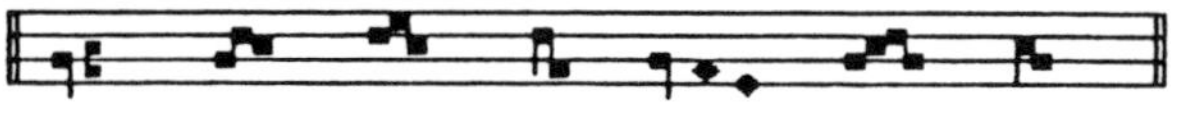

Diapason supra et infra duobus deficiens tonis; tropo tribuit imperfectionem

Demonstratio tetrardi imperfecti [Ex. 63]

Diapason cui tonus superius abest; ea in parte imperfectionem facit tonum

Demonstratio plagalis tetrardi imperfecti [Ex. 64]

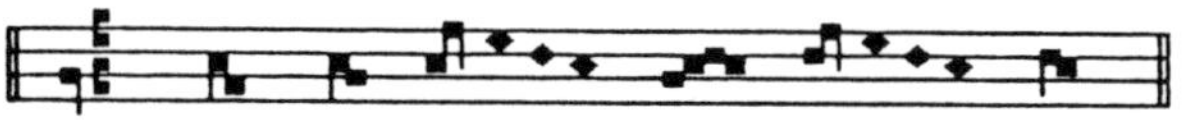

Diapason supra et infra duobus deficiens tonis; tropum facit a perfectione distare

[138] Hos, autem qui supra diapason aliquid videntur addere, eo quod perfectam servant formam et aliquid plus addiciunt, plusquamperfectos in autenticis merito nominamus. [139] Quos autem in plagalibus infra fines ubi eorum ultimus ex diapason perficitur terminus tonum vel semitonium et cetera, contingit deponere etiam dicimus plusquamperfectos. [140] Supra igitur autenticus dicitur plusquamperfectus, sed infra plagalis et non supra, quia in ea parte mixtus appellatur, ut nunc dicetur. [Exx. 65–66]

Demonstratio autentici plusquamperfecti

Diapason in inferiori termino adiuncta cum tono

Demonstratio plagalis autentici plusquamperfecti

Diapason in inferiori termino adiuncta cum tono

[141] Qui autem autentici infra tonum, semitonium vel ditonum et cetera deponunt, eo quod cum suo plagali miscentur, appellantur mixti; plagalibus vero quorum ascensui vel diapente aliquid supponitur, eo quod cum suo autentico mixturam faciunt, etiam mixtorum nomina tribuimus. [142] Inferius igitur est mixtus autenticus, cuius nomen plagalis superius tenet ad horum differentiam mixtorum, quorum species cum aliorum speciebus commisceri videntur nempe appellantur commixti. [143] Potest enim uniuscuisque tropi cum alterius cuius(cum)que specie unaquaeque species commisceri. [144] Eorum demonstrationes, ut clare videantur quae dicta sunt, hic infra ponemus, ut unius demonstratione singulorum notitia habeatur. [Exx. 67–68]

Demonstratio autentici mixti

Diapason in termino inferiori adiuncta ditono

Demonstratio plagalis mixti

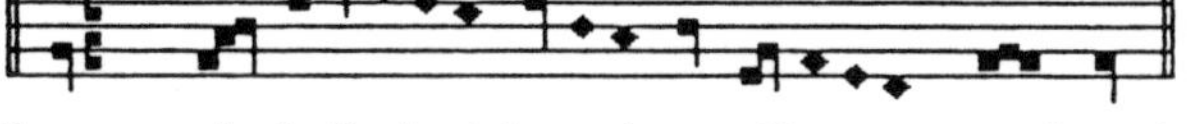

Diapason in inferiori termino adiuncta semitonio

[145] De commixtis autem speciebus in tropis hoc notandum acci-

pimus quod tropi sic ad invicem sunt commixti quod vix unus reperiri contingat qui propriis duntaxat speciebus sit formatus. [146] Ad cognoscendum cuius toni sint antiphonae quae ascensum seu descensum sui tropi non complent, inspicere debes finem antiphonae et principium de saeculorum et de hoc dantur hi versus, scilicet,

[147] Re la vult primus, re fa retinetque secundus,
[148] Per sextam mi fa terno, quarto dato mi la,
[149] Fa fa fert quintus, fa la praebet tibi sextus,
[150] Ut sol septenus, ut fa captatque supremus.

[151] De cantibus qui propter eorum ascensum non sunt autentici et propter eorum descensum non sunt plagales

[152] Notandum est quod inveniuntur multi cantus qui propter suas brevitates et compositiones non possunt iudicari autentici nec plagales, quia non habent ascensum ut autentici, nec descensum ut plagales. [153] Unde huiusmodi cantus sunt iudicandi per eorum cordas tali modo, quod si habent plures notulas in numero supra ipsam cordam quam sub eadem corda, tales cantus sunt autentici. [154] Si vero plures notulae fuerint inferius quam superius erunt plagales. [155] Advertendum tamen est quod notae quae situatae sunt in corda, non debent computari in numero cum illis, quae sunt superius vel inferius. [156] Et nota quod corda primi et secundi toni est in manu in digito auriculari F fa ut gravi et in linea. [157] Corda tertii et quarti toni est in G sol re ut, gravi et in spatio. [158] Corda quinti et sexti toni est in A la mi re, acuto et in linea. [159] Corda septimi et octavi toni est in B fa ♮ mi, acuto et in spatio.

Sancta Brigida

[160] Clericorum cantus non sit remissus, non fractus, non dissolutus sed honestus et gravis et uniformis et per omnia humilis. [161] Psalmodia plus redoleat suavitatem mentis, humilitatem quam et devotionem quam aliquam ostentationem. [162] Nam non vacat a culpa animus

quando cantantem plus delectat nota quam res quaecanitur, omninoque abominabile est Deo quando vocis elevatio plus fit propter audientes quam propter Deum.

[163] Hic modus cantandi revelatus fuit a Domino Jesu Christo Sanctae Brigidae viduae, ut habetur in suo volumine et in Libro Extravaganti cap. iiii.

CRITICAL NOTES

Plate I. T499–09: Sentences 1–8 appear in the palm of the hand; no inscription appears above or beneath the staff, although T505 displays the printer's initials, I B S, beneath the staff. T 499: no musical staff. R587: inscription beneath the staff, *SCANDIT DESCENDIT.* C540A & B lack Notes 5–8 in the palm.

[1]R564–97: Sentences 1–8 are moved to after 38 below; the topic sentence is rephrased, *Sciendum tamen, quod proprietas in . . .*, and 9–16 are deleted. C566 does likewise, but begins *Et proprietas in.* R587–88: The title is followed by a chapter title, *De Instrumento manus, notis, & vocibus in ea descriptis. Cap. 1.* Marchetto's original: *Est enim proprietas in cantu derivatio plurium vocum ab uno et eodem . . .*

[2]Sources after 1509: *notitia habenda.*

[3]Sources after 1505: *vox ut.* Ugolino lacks *videlicet, re mi fa sol la* and *scilicet, re mi fa sol la.*

[6]R523–67, C538–49: the final clef sign follows *pro.* C566: final clef sign follows *quo.* Sources after 1512: *♯ acutum pro quo tale signum.* Marchetto: *sunt duae, scilicet F grave et c acutum.*

[9]T499–09, R564, C566, R576–97 lack the heading *Versus* and 9–16, giving them after *hi versus* (sentence 146)

[16]R523–60, C540B, R567 repeat the title, *Compendium musice,* after this line.

Plate II. Omitted in T499–09, C550–66.

[17]C513: *in inprimas.* R564: *inprimas et videlicet.* R587: *et gravibus.*

[19]T499, C513–66, R523–76: *vocabulo y. Gamma.* R587–88: *ut* in place of *G.*

[20]Sources after 1509: *sumpsisse.* R587–88: *initio a Grecis.*

[21–25]Marchetto: *et ideo dicitur gravis quia in illo inferiori loco primitus est formata; et tales in constitutione manus sunt septem, scilicet A, ♯, C, D, E, F, et G. Acutae dicuntur eo quod acutum reddunt sonum respectu gravium praedictarum; formantur enim in superiori loco, scilicet in voce gutturis . . .*

[23]The use of lower case letters for pitches in the *acutus* and *superacutus* registers occurs only in T499–05 and parts of R576.

[25]R576–97: *est* lacking.

[26–27]Marchetto: *Superacutae dicuntur eo quod super praedictas acutas sonum reddunt, et ratio est quia formantur in excelsiori loco, scilicet in voce capitis.*

[27]T499–09, C513–49, R523–67 delete *omni depictam hanc.*

[28]T509: *tibi* in place of *ibi.* R554–64, *R569–97,* C566: *queue littere.* C513: *D* in place of *B.* C566: *cognascas, in manu ipsa perpende est A.* R587–88: preceded by a chapter title, *De Literas Mvsicalibus & clauibus. Cap. 2.*

[29]R569 adds *prout in hac subiecta figura patet.* C513, R554–97, C566: *acutis spatio sunt.* R554–64, R576, R579B–97 conclude: *prout in hac figura patet.*

[30–36]Deleted in C550.

[30]C513, R523–97 lack *quod.* C566, R576–97: *debere* in place of *debet.*

[32]R585A & B, R596 lack *per.*

[33]C566: *enim B rotundum accidentale, et quod accidentale est, non est.*

[34]T499–05: *asperius.* C566 lacks *qui . . . intenitur.* R569 lacks *B.*

[37]C549: *ponuntur, ex.*

[41]R585A & B, R596–97: *B subgravi.* C566: *in manus.* C513–49, R523–55, R564–69, C566: *F gravi.*

[42]All sources before 1550: *G gravi.* C566: *G sub gravi.*

[43]R569: *E gravi.*

[44]R523–55, C538–49, R564–97, C566: *F acuto.*

[45]C550: *A superacuto.*

[46]C550: *D superacuto.*

[47]C513–66, R523–69: *G superacuto.* C550: single letters *E* and ♯.

[48]R587–88: the caption concludes, *Cap. 3.*

[49]C550 lacks *vel fieri potest.* T499–05: *diumse que quidem;* all other sources: *divise que quidem;* the above reading is taken from Marchetto.

[50–60]C550 deletes 50, 52–55, Exx. 1–19, and 60; 51 begins *Nam ubi sola . . .*; 59 is followed by the advice: *Quas mutationes a magistro te docente, addisces.*

[51]R564, R569–76, R579B–97 lack *maius.* Sources after 1510: *sunt istae duae.* R554–60, R567: *voces de b.b. mi.* R564: *voces de b. la ♯ mi.* C550, R564: *nam ubi: in B.*

[52–60] R564, C566, R569–97 delete 52–55, Exx. 1–19, and sentence 60. The following replaces 52–55: *Preterea notare debemus, quod mutatio fieri debet duobus casibus* [R588: *in duobus*; C566: *duobus de causis*] *scilicet, quando cantus transgreditur vocem la unius proprietatis per duas voces, seu notas, et quandoque per unam tantum. Et quando sub voce, seu nota, ut per unam tantum descendit. Primo modo mutatur sol, vel la, in re, et vocatur mutatio ascendens. Secundo modo mutatur re, vel ut in la, et vocatur mutatio descendens. Exemplum primi.* [R588: Notes 3–7 a second higher.]

Exemplum secundi

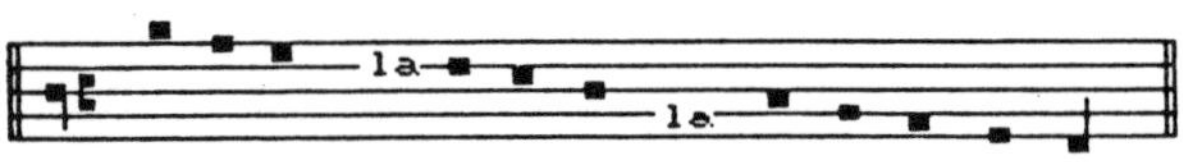

Anima advertendum tamen est, quod mutatio ascendens fit semper in re, mutatio descendens fit semper in la, et hoc quando cantus per gradus procedit, secus autem si per gradus non progrederetur, quia tunc mutatio effectu non fit, sed intelligitur facienda, prout in exemplo sequenti videri potest. [C566: A inserted after Note 3; Note 9 deleted; 13 reads d; 17–27 read e, f; 29–31 read d, e, d, c, B, A. R587: Notes 4–16 a second lower; 31–33 read c, d, e.]

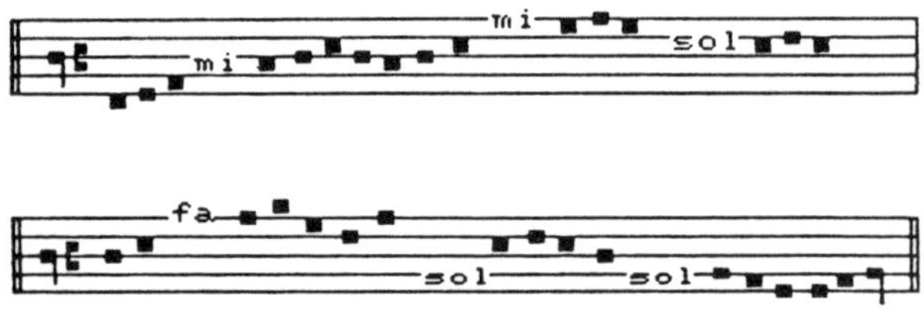

[54] C513, R523, C549: *ascendo* and *descendo.*

[56] C566: *Mutatio tunc non debet.*

[59] T509: *armonicum.* R569–97 lack final *et.* R537: *B duro.*

Ex. 1. R530 inserts g after Note 19; last two notes read G, c.

Exx. 1–4. T499–09: captions read *locus mutationis.*

Ex. 2. C538: Notes 16–17 a second lower. C540A: Note 4 missing.

Ex. 3. R530 inserts b after Note 15; 17 deleted. C540A: F-clef a third lower. R567: Notes 4–5 deleted; 13 a second lower. R554–60: Notes 14–15 a second higher.

Ex. 4. T509, C513–49: B-flat given one space higher. T505–09, C549: Note 18 missing. R560: Note 2 a second higher; 4, 16–17 a third higher. R567: Notes 1–2, 4 a second higher; 20 a second lower. C540A & B: Notes 1–3 read f, g, f; Notes 7–9 read c', f. R548–55: Notes 2–4 read g, e, g. R555: Note 5 deleted; Notes 12–15 a second higher; this edition notates accidentals inconsistently, using b or ⊏ for B-flat; b or ♭ for B-naturals in the examples.

Ex. 5. C513: no B-flat in signature. C540A: Notes 7–8 omitted. C549: f, e inserted before the final note. R555–60: e, a, g, a, c', g, a, e. R567 registered a second higher.

Exx. 5–6. C538–40B, R549: double bar separating these occurs four notes too late; those four notes are a third lower.

Exx. 5–7. T499–09: *G graue et primum* beneath the staff.

Ex. 6. Ugolino lacks Notes 2 and 18. C540A: ♯ a third lower. R560: Notes 1–2 a second lower; 5 a second higher; last note repeated. C549: caption reads ♯ *et*; Notes 2–5 missing.

Ex. 7. C540A: No B-flat in signature; Note 7 a second higher. R554–60, R567: Notes 8–9 a second lower; last two notes missing.

Ex. 8. R530: Notes 4 and 5 a second lower. C540A: B-flat. R548: Note 2 a second lower; 8–9 a third lower. R554, R567: Notes 2–7 read g, e, f, g, f, d; *G acutum* beneath the staff. R555: Note 1 a second higher; 8–9 a third lower. R560: Notes 3–7 read e, g, a, f, d. R537: Notes 3–6 a third lower.

Ex. 9. C513–49 insert g after Note 9.

Ex. 10. C513–49: Note 4 a second higher. R560: Notes 2–5 and 8–9 a second higher. Ugolino inserts d' after Note 7.

Ex. 11. R530: Notes 1 and 2 read a, f. R523–60, C538–49: the caption is preceded by *Sequitur de septimo mutationis loco.* R567: Notes 6–9 read b-flat, c', b-flat, a. Ugolino gives g, b-flat, d' for Notes 1–4; lacks Note 8; and adds g, f at the end.

Ex. 12. R554–60, R567: Notes 1–3 a second lower. R567: flat sign a third lower; Notes 7–10 a second higher.

Exx. 12–13, 15–16. T499–09 and Ugolino: captions lack *acutae.* Ugolino: *variationum* in place of *mutationis.*

Ex. 13. R555: Note 12 reads b, c', b. R554: registered a second higher. R567: b precedes Note 1; last note a second higher.

Ex. 14. R567: Note 6 repeated; # deleted.

Ex. 16. R555, R567: order of Notes 4–5 reversed. R567: # deleted; Notes 10–12 read a, b, a. Ugolino inserts e after Note 9.

Ex. 17. C540A: C-clef a third lower. R567: Note 1 a second higher; 16 deleted. Ugolino lacks Note 1.

Ex. 18. R537–67: Notes 6–8 a second higher. R537–60: Note 16 a second higher. R567: flat sign omitted; Notes 16 and 18 a second lower. R554–60, R567: C-clef a third higher.

Ex. 19. C540A: final note is c'. R567; Notes 3–10 a second lower. Ugolino lacks Note 1.

Exx. 19–21. T499–09: *G secundum et acutum* beneath the staff. T499–09 and Ugolino: captions lack *acutae.*

Ex. 20. R537–60: Note 1 a third higher. R560: Notes 4–8 read a, e', a, g, d. R567: # in signature; e', g', f', a', d'', c'', a', f', d'.

Ex. 21. C513: Note 10 reads c'. R560: last note a second too low. R567: no accidentals; Notes 2–3 read g', a'; 10–11 read g', d'. Only T499–09 give a caption, *B mollis # quadri.* Ugolino lacks *mutationis.*

Ex. 22. R530: 5 is g'; Note 7 is b', b', g'. C540A: Notes 6–8 read b', a'. R554–60, R567: Notes 8–9 a second lower. R554–60: Note 1 a second lower. R560: Note 8 a second lower. R567: Note 1 reads c', e'. T499–09 and Ugolino: caption lacks *acutae.* Ugolino: *variationum* in place of *mutationis.*

Ex. 23. C540B: Note 6 deleted. R548–60, R567: B-flat. R554–60, R567: Notes 5–9 read d'', g', g', d', c'. R567: Note 1 a second lower. Ugolino: Note 5 a second lower.

Exx. 23–24. T499–09 and Ugolino: captions lack *superacutae.*

Ex. 24. R537: e'' inserted after Note 5. R548: Notes 6–14 read d'', b', d'', c'', b', a', g', d', f', e. R560: Notes 1–5 a second lower; 6–14 read c'', g', c'', b', g', f', f', c, f', e'. R554–55, R567: Notes 6–14 read d'', a', d'', c'', a', g', g', d', f', e'.

Ex. 25. R548–60 registered a second lower. R567: e', b', a', a', b', b', a, d'', d'', c'', a', b', b', a', e', f', e'.

Ex. 26. T509: Square note in place of first flat. R523–48, R530: F precedes Note 1. C540A & B: Note 11 a second higher. R554–60: e', f', a', b'-flat, c'', c'', b'-natural, d'', c'', d'', d'', c'', b'-flat, f', f', e'. R567: e', f', a', b', c'', c'', b', c'', e'', d'', e'', e'', d'', c'', f', f', e'. C538–40A, C549 lack first flat.

[61]All editions give the caption, *De coniunctionibus vocum que sint.* The caption as shown above is from Marchetto. R587–88: Caption labelled *Cap. 4.*

[62–63]Marchetto: *Syllaba in musica est tonus, semitonium, ditonus, et semiditonus, quae consonantiarum membra proprie nuncupantur. Isidorus: Toni et semitonia sunt particularae consonantiarum.*

[65]R576–97: *pluries in manu.* R548–69: *pluribus in manu.*

[69]R587–88: Caption labelled *Cap. 5.*

[70]R576–97 lack *est.*

[71]C550–66: *inter D et E . . . inter F et G et econverso, inter G et A et econverso.* C540A & B, R548–67, R576–97: *A et ♯ et . . . a D ad E et . . . ab F et G et . . .* T505 lacks *ut hic patet exemplo.*

Ex. 27. C550–66 precede this with pitches G, A. C540B: Notes 3–4 a second lower.

Exx. 27–31. R555: registered a second lower.

[72]R564–97, C566 lack *minus.* R576–97: *mediate.* R587–88: Caption labelled *Cap. 6.*

[73]C566: *quasi imperfectum.*

[74]C566: *toni maior.* R587: *intelligenti in.* R564–97: *minor* deleted.

[75]C566: *inter A et B. . . inter B et C et econverso . . .* T499–09, C513–49, and R523–67 lack *quadratum.* R567: *Ad et b rotundum.*

Ex. 35. R555: B-flat.

[76]R523–97 and C540A & B lack the heading. R588: heading labelled *Cap. 7.* R530 heading, *Ditonus.*

[77]R569–97: *integra est eius.* Sources after 1505: *tonis compositio.* Ugolino: *tonos duos.*

[78]Ugolino and C550–66 delete the last four words. R588: *ut hic sequitur.* Ugolino: *Dicitur enim.*

Ex. 36. R567: Notes 4–5 deleted. R569: Notes 6–7 precede 4. R588: Notes 6–7 follow Note 4.

Exx. 36–38. R587: *Cap. 7. Ditono* replaces the captions.

Ex. 37. C549: Note 1 a second lower. R560–97: *F G* beneath the staff.

Ex. 38. R560–64, R576–97: Notes 6–7 deleted. R585A & B: F-clef.

[79] *Sic,* no heading introduces this paragraph, except for R588, which gives *De semiditono. Cap. 8.*

[80]C566: *ditono.* Ugolino: *imperfectus tonus et non plenus . . .*

[81]R564–97 and C566: *minoris semitonii.* Only T499–09 provide *ditoni.*

[82]C513 lacks *ut hic sequitur.* R576–97: *semiditoni imperfectum.* Ugolino lacks last three words.

Ex. 39. R587: *Cap. 8.* precedes the caption.

Exx. 39–44. R567: no letters beneath the staff.

Ex. 40. R576–97: Notes 3–8 read f, d, f, f, e. R567: Notes 4–5 deleted.

Ex. 41. C540A & B: Notes 1 and 10 a second higher. R555: Note 10 a second higher.

[83]R564, C566 lack *minus.* R587–88: caption labelled *Cap. 9.*

[84]R564–97: *per* in place of *de.*

[85]T505: *necere.*

Exx. 42–44. R576–97: in C-clef and an octave higher.

Ex. 42. R564: Notes 1–11 a second higher. R587–88 give a caption, *De tribus speciebus diatessaron. Cap. 10.*

Ex. 43. Sources from 1513 to 1566: *B F* beneath the staff. C540A & B: Notes 7–8 a second higher. R567: Notes 4–5 missing. R576–97: Notes 11–12 read d, a. R554–69: Ex. 43 is missing, Ex. 44 being printed twice.

[91]R523, R548: *Diapente ex.* R548–97 and sources before 1539: *consonantia quinque.* R548–69: caption lacks *De.* R587–88: caption labelled *Cap. 11.* R564–97: *continens* in place of *minus contentibus facta.*

[92]R564–97: *per* in place of *de.* C566: *pente quod est.*

[93]C566: *est qui retineat.* R579A–97: *diatessaron tono.*

[94]T505: *reperte.* R585A, R597 lack *et.*

[95]C499: *diatessaron et tono procedit.* C505: *diatessaron ex tono procedit.* R548–97, C566: *fa, sol, re, mi.*

[96]R564–97, C566: *fa, sol, re.*

Exx. 45–48. R587–88 give a caption, *De Quatuor speciebus Diapente. Cap. 12.*

Ex. 45. R579B–97: Notes 6–7 read f, d.

Ex. 46. C550–66: *G D* beneath the staff. R579B: Note 14 a second lower.

Ex. 47. R555: Note 7 a second higher. R579A: Note 7 a third lower.

Ex. 48. T499–09: final note missing. R564: *G G* beneath the staff. R567: Note 7 a second lower. C540A & B: Note 7 missing.

[98]R564–97: *minora* omitted. R587–88: caption labelled *Cap. 13.*

[99]R564–97: *per* in place of *de.* C550–66: *pason quod est.*

[101]C550 ends after this sentence, adding *Finis.* R588: *quinta ab C.*

[102]R569–97: *Tropus sive tonus modus* and *pneumatum.* Ugolino: *ordinatis speciebus;* T499–05: *ordinationis speciebus;* sources after 1506: *ordinatione specie.* Sources after 1510: *constitutio* as the final word. R564: *diapente a diatessaron.* C566 lacks *ex.* R587–88: caption labelled *Cap. 14.* Ugolino: *per arsyn et thesyn;* his caption reads *tropi sive.*

[103]All editions except R554–97 mistakenly read *tropum* in place of *protum.* Ugolino: *Hinc est quod Graeci, ut dictum est, quatuor tropos antedictos sub quatuor vocum cognitione.*

[104–107]Rephrased in C566: *In voce enim re et D prima sibi coniuncta littera cum suo subiugali finitur. In mi voce et E prima littera tertius modus cum suo subiugali finalem sedem acquirit. In voce fa atque scilicet littera prima quintus modus et sextus modus eius subiugalis est terminatus. Sed in voce sol et littera G que est prima septimus cum suo subiugali est conflatus.*

[107]T499–09: *subiugali suo.* Ugolino, final word is *confinitus.*

[108]R564–97: *formationi.* R588: *sunt: in eis.*

[109]Sources after 1505: *ut patebit exemplo.* C566 deletes last three words. Ugolino: *tropi octo* and he concludes, *demonstratio patet hic.*

[110]R587–88: labelled *Cap. 15.*

[111–146]Deleted in C566.

[112]Ugolino: *formam suam; specie et coniunctione diapason constituentibus, producunt enim; species, ut iam dictum est, quae sunt; D primo reque secunda, ubi ipse tropus cum suo subiugali. . .*

[113]Ugolino: *Huius ergo plagalis forma est in D.*

[114]Sources other than T499–09, C540A & B: *qui forma.* R530–69: *specierum autentice.* R576–97: *specie autentice.* T499–09, C513–49: *specierum autente.* Ugolino lacks last live words.

[115]R537–64: *et est diatessaron.* R567: *re la diatessaron.* R585A & B, R596–97: *la ex diatessaron.* Ugolino concludes, *ut hic demonstratur.*

Ex. 49. R530: Note 12 reads e. R560: Notes 9–12 a second lower. R564–69: Notes 15–21 read g, a, g, f, e. R579B–97: *a diatessaron* beneath the staff. R576–97: Notes 15–19 read g, a, g, f.

Exx. 49–50. R587–88 give a different caption, *De Duplici demonstratione proti perfecti, et plagali proti perfecti. Cap. 16.*

Ex. 50. T509, C513–40B, R530–97 lack Note 1. C540A & B: caption reads *imperfecti.* C549 inserts d before Note 1. R564: Notes 1–7 registered a second higher. R569–97: Notes 9–18 read a second higher; d added at the end.

[116]Sources after 1505: *formam suam.*

[117]Ugolino: *vocem suam.*

[118]C513, R576: *tropi seu modi.* Ugolino concludes, *ut hic.*

[119]R564; *formam utriusque.* R567: *diapente et diapente et diatessaron.*

Ex. 51. R537–97 repeat last pitch. C549: Notes 1–4 a third lower. R564 registered a second lower. R567: Note 8 a second lower. R569: *et* missing beneath the staff. R585A & B, R596–97: Note 1 reads f; Notes 7–10 read a, c', f', f'.

Exx. 51–52. R587–88 supplies a caption, *De duplici demonstratione Deuteri perfecti, et Plagalis Deuteri perfecti. Cap. 17.* T499: These two examples are mounted upside down on one staff.

Ex. 52. C513–38, C540B: Notes 1–4 read c, e, f, e; *coniuncta superius* beneath the staff. R523–37: Notes 7 to end: e, b, g, f, e, e, d, B, d, e, d, e, e, e, f, e, e. R548–54, R569 do likewise, but last note is f. R567 does likewise, but Note 1 reads A, f; last note is e, f. R587–88: Note 1 reads f. R555: Notes 7 to end: b, e, b, g, f, e, e, d, B, d, e, d, e, e, e, f, e, f, g, f. R560 does likewise, but lacks last two notes. R564 attempted the same, but registered it a second higher. R576, R587–88: Notes 7 to end: e, a, f, e, d, e, d, c, d, e, d, e, e, e, f, e, e. R585A & B, R596–97: f, a, g, a, a, a, e, a, f, e, d, e, d, c, d, e, d, e, e, e, e, d, e; R579A & B do likewise, but Notes 2–6 read g, a, g, a, b-flat, and Notes 21–22 read f, e. R530: *coniuncta superius* beneath the staff.

[121]R579A–97 lack *ex.*

[122]Ugolino: *fine ac.* R560: last word is *constituerunt.*

[125]R554–97: *supra diapente convertitur.* Ugolino: *in ceteris. Nam utriusque.*

[126]R564–97 lack *ex.* R523–30: *et* in place of *ex.* Ugolino: *Huius ergo;* last five words: *ut ex inferiori demonstratione constat.* T499–05: *ut ex inferiori de-*

monstratione monstratur.

Ex. 53. R523, R554: Notes 8–10 read f, c', f'. R530: Notes 3–12 read d', f', f , c', f', d', c'. R523–97: B-flat in signature and final pitch repeated. R537: Notes 8–10 read e', c', f', d', c'. R555, R579A, R587–88: Notes 8–10 read f', e, c', e'. R579B does likewise, but Note 9 reads f. R548, R560, R567–69: Notes 8–10 read f, c', e'. R564 attempted the same, but registered it a second lower. R576: Notes 8–10 read f', e, b'-flat, e'. R585A & B, R596–97: Note 7 reads d', e', f, b-flat, c'; pitches a, g, f added after Note 10. R585–97: *et* lacking beneath the staff.

Exx. 53–54. R587–88 give a caption, *De duplici demonstratione triti perfecti, et plagalis triti perfecti. Cap. 18.*

Ex. 54. R588 adds g at end. R548–60: Notes 11–12 a second lower. R530–97 repeat final pitch. R564: registered a second lower. R548–69: Note 17 a second lower. C540A and sources before 1514 lack the last note. R537, R585A & B, R596–97: Note 16 a second higher.

[127]Printed sources before 1569 lack *est.* T499–05: *septius; sepius* in all other sources; *septimus* in Ugolino's original. Ugolino: *ultimus est in ordine.*

[130]R530–60, C538–40A, R567: *ideo in eo* C. R564, R569–97: *ideo in re G.* Ugolino: *ut ex hac demonstratione constat.*

[131]*qui quarta* in sources other than Ugolino and R576–79A, R585A–97.

[132]R564–97: *supponitur, sed in.* Sources after 1512: *ipsa* in place of *ista.* Ugolino: *servatur. Hi namque eo quod unius sunt compacti materiae in eodem fundamento atque fine modo et ordine habent convenire, quoniam G primum utriusque fundamentum et finis est.*

[133]R587: *et re ut inferius.* Ugolino: *Ipsius ergo plagalis forma . . . ut inferius demonstratur.*

Ex. 55. R523–97: in F-clef (basically transposed down a fifth) and final pitch repeated. R523–37: c, g, f, g, b, a, g, g, c', b, a, g, g, f, e, c, d, f, e, d, c, c. R564–76, R585A & B, R596–97 do likewise, but Note 16 reads d. R579B, R587–88 do likewise, but mistakenly in C-clef and R587–88, final note, is a. R548–60, R567 do likewise, but Notes 6–7 read g, f; 14–16 read a, g, c.

Exx. 55–56. R587–88 give a caption, *De demonstratione tetarti perfecti, et plagalis tetarti perfecti. Cap. 19.*

Ex. 56. R523–79B, R587–88: final pitch repeated. R549: registered a second lower. R555, R567: Note 14 a second higher. R579A: b inserted after Note 14. R576, R587 lack Note 9; *perfectum* in caption. R585A & B, R596–97: d', g', e', d', e', g', g', f', a', g', f', e', d', d', a , d', c', d', e', d', d' (basically transposed up a fifth).

[134]R588 supplies a caption, *Diapason ex diapente, cui infra adiungitur superius diatessaron. Cap. 20.*

[135]T499–09 lack the second *ex.* R569: *pneumatum.*

[136]Ugolino: *attingat.*

[137]T499–09: *indicabitur.* R585A, R597 lack *est.* Ugolino lacks last three words.

Ex. 57. R530 inserts b, a after Note 5. R554–60, R567: Notes 8–10 a second higher. R585A–97: Notes 16–17 a second higher.

Exx. 57–64. R587–88 supplies a caption, *De variis Diapason consonantiis. Cap. 21.*

Ex. 58. R585A, R596–97: Notes 3 and 4 a second lower. R587: Note 10 a second lower. R569–97: Note 8 missing.

Ex. 59. C513–49, R530–79B, R587 lack Note 7. Sources after 1506: order of Notes 12–13 reversed. R555, R576: Note 12 missing. R555, R576–79A, R588: Note 14 reads a. C540A, R585A & B, R588–97: Notes 7–8 read c', c'. R567: Note 1 a second higher.

Ex. 60. C513–40B, R530, R554–67, R576–79A, R585A–97: Notes 17–18 a third lower. R555, R567: Note 1 a second lower. R560: Notes 15–16 a third lower. C540A, R564–97: Notes 5–6 a second higher. R585A & B, R597: Note 14 a second lower; final note is g, f.

Ex. 61. R530 adds a at end. R537–79B: final pitch repeated. R576, R588: Notes 4–6 a second higher. R564, R569–97: Notes 11–12 a second higher. R587–88 add e at end. R587: *diapason inferiori* beneath the staff. R596–97: a inserted after Note 15. Ugolino lacks Note 1.

Ex. 62. R530–97: last note repeated. R567: order of Notes 7–8 reversed. R579A–97: Note 8 a second lower. C513 and sources after 1539 lack *duobus* beneath the staff.

Ex. 63. R567: order of Notes 14–15 reversed. R585A & B, R596–97: Note 7 a second lower.

Ex. 64. R576–79B, R587–88: Note 14 a second higher. R579A, R587–88: Note 2 a second lower.

[139]R564–97 lack *ex.*

Ex. 65. R530: Note 7 reads e'. R555: last note reads e, f, e. R560: Note 1 a second lower. R567: Notes 13–15 read g, f, g. R585A & B, R596–97: Note 18 a second lower. R554–97: last note a second higher. Sources after 1529: *superiori* replaces *inferiori* beneath the staff. R588: Note 7 reads g. Ugolino lacks last note.

Ex. 66. R537–54: Notes 17–18 a second higher. R548: Note 1 a second higher. R555: Notes 17–24 a second higher. R560–69: Note 16 a second lower; 21–24 a second higher. R564–69: Notes 1–5 read A, B, c, d, c. R576–97: Notes 4–5 read c'; 16 a second lower. R587: Notes 1–4 read B, c, d, c; 13–18 read c, B, c. R564–97: *termino inferiori* beneath the staff. R588: Notes 2–5 read B, c, d, c. Ugolino lacks last note.

Ex. 67. C513–40B, R537–55, R588: Note 3 repeated. R530: Notes 4–5 read f, a. C540A & B: Notes 1–2 a third higher. R537–97, C538–49: Note 18 deleted. C549: Note 4 reads b, d'. R560–97: Notes 11–12 a second higher. R567: Notes 1–4 read f, a, a, g, b. R587: Notes 1–2 read f, a, a. R560–85B, R596–97: Notes 1–3 read f, a, a, b. R576–97: *tono* replaces *ditono* beneath the staff. R588: Notes 1–2 a second higher. Ugolino lacks last note.

Ex. 68. R564–87, R596–97: Notes 5–7, 18–19, 23–25 a second higher.

R548–60: Note 9 a second higher. R548–60, R567–79B, R587–88: Note 11 a second lower. R569: Note 10 a second higher. R576, R579B, R587: Note 12 a second lower. R585A & B, R596–97: Note 12 a third lower. R560: Notes 5–7 a second higher. R587–88: Note 22 a second higher. R576–85B, R596–97: Note 22 a second lower. Ugolino lacks last note.

[145]Ugolino: *tropis speciebus.*

[146]C566: *Unde ad . . . sint antiphone, inspicere.*

[147]C513, R523, C549, C560: *primus, et cetera ut supra in principio*, then omit to sentence 151. C540A & B read to *primus,* then skip to sentence 151.

[150]T499–09, R564–97 follow this with lines 13–16; T499–09 then end.

[151–158]Deleted in C566.

[152–154]Marchetto: *Sunt nonulli cantus qui a fine eorum ad diapente et non ultra ascendunt, et per talem interruptionem quae in authentico et in plagali cadere potest, nec infra a fine aliquid descendunt, nec habent diapente continuam, nec utuntur diapente communi, quae pluries in uno cantu repercussa facit ipsum subjugalem, ut superius dictum est; nunc talis cantus cui attribui debet, authentico an plagali? Dicendum est quod tales cantus judicandi sunt per chordam eorum, ita videlicet quod si notae quae sunt supra eorum chordam sunt plures quam illae quae sunt infra, authenticus erit, et e converso . . .*

[159]R523–30: text ends before the heading *Sancta Brigida,* closing by adding the phrase *Explicit Compendium musice.* R576, R579B, R587: *in B la.* R537–67 insert *Explicit Compendium musice* but then continue.

[160]C566, R579A, R585A–97: *gravis, uniformis.* R587: *sit pressus.* C540A & B: caption reads *De Sancta Brigida.*

[163]R564–97 lack this sentence, appending instead the phrase *Finit Compendium musice.* C566 also lacks this sentence, appending *Explicit compendium musice.*